D1135496

TAROT

Discover the Mysteries of the Future with Tarot

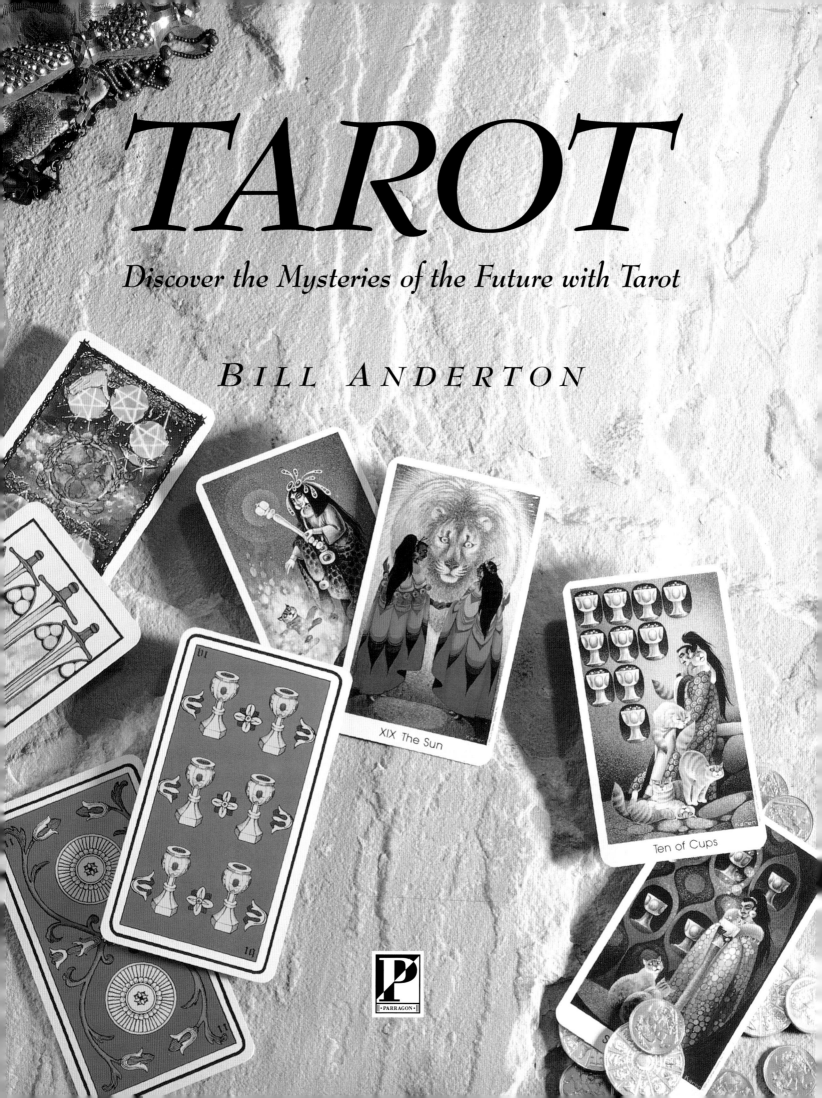

TAROT

Discover the Mysteries of the Future with Tarot

BILL ANDERTON

XIX The Sun

Ten of Cups

First Published in Great Britain by
Parragon Books Limited
Units 13-17, Avonbridge Industrial Estate
Atlantic Road, Avonmouth, Bristol BS11 9QD
United Kingdom

Designed and produced by
Touchstone
Old Chapel Studio, Plain Road
Marden, Tonbridge Kent TN12 9LS
United Kingdom

ISBN 0-75251-718-X

Printed in Italy

Photography Credits:

(*Abbreviations: r = right, l = left, t = top, b = below*)

The Image Bank: pages 14, 15, 16*t*, 16*l*, 17, 19, 22, 25, 29,
74, 84, 90, 91*t*, 91*b*, 92*l*.

Images Colour Library Ltd: pages 7, 8*t*, 8*b*, 9, 10, 11, 13,
26, 27*t*, 27*r*, 28, 71.

Robin MacDougall Photographics: pages 1, 2-3, 6, 12, 18,
24, 30, 70, 78, 81, 83, 85, 86, 88, 95.

Telegraph Colour Library: page 82.

Touchstone: pages 4, 5, 21, 23, 77, 92*t*, 92-93, 94.

Illustrations from tarot decks listed below and published by
U.S. Games Systems, Inc. CT 06902 USA, reproduced by
permission. Further reproduction prohibited.

Aquarian Tarot Deck, © 1970 U.S. Games Systems, Inc.

Golden Dawn Tarot Deck, © 1977 U.S. Games Systems, Inc.

Hanson-Roberts Tarot Deck, © 1985 U.S. Games Systems, Inc.

Morgan-Greer Tarot Deck, © 1979 U.S. Games Systems, Inc.

1JJ Swiss Tarot Deck, © 1974 U.S. Games Systems, Inc.

Oswald Wirth Tarot Deck, © U.S. Games Systems, Inc.

Pierpont Morgan-Bergamo Visconti-Sforza Tarrochi Deck,
© 1975 U.S. Games Systems, Inc.

Sacred Rose Tarot Deck, © 1982 U.S. Games Systems, Inc.

Tarot of the Cat People, © 1985 U.S. Games Systems, Inc.

Contents

Story of the Tarot

This book will make it as easy as possible for you to understand how to use the Tarot cards. With it, you will be able to learn how the Tarot works, what all the cards mean and how to do an interpretation for yourself or for your friends. To achieve this, the book has been carefully designed so that you can read right through it or pick from the bits that suit you. Then you will find that it is a handy reference work containing concise information to help you develop your skill in reading the cards.

The way this is achieved is by giving you in this chapter a summary of the whole book – of the Tarot story. This will present you with a rounded introduction that tells you what the Tarot is all about and how it is used. This is followed by in-depth information about the Tarot pack and how it is structured. The next chapters give you brief information about the meaning of each card followed by a fuller interpretation of each one. The final chapters tell you how to prepare and conduct an effective Tarot reading.

Tarot Cards for Fortune Telling & Fun

More than any other system for fortune telling, the Tarot cards carry an aura of mystery about them. There is no doubt that their history is a long one, going back so far in time that it is impossible to be certain about their origin. One thing is certain, however, and that is the popularity of Tarot divination, witnessed by the great number of different decks which are available today.

Some of these decks are quite old in their design and many of them are modern, the artwork and symbols depicted on them being inspired by many diverse ideas. Whatever the name on a Tarot deck, whether it be The Medicine Woman Tarot, The Enchanted Tarot, or Tarot of the Cat People, the method for reading the cards is the same and it is this method which we will be exploring.

The Tarot Story

The invention of the Tarot cards has been ˙attributed to various sources. Some have seen in the word 'tarot' a corruption of the name Thoth, the ancient Egyptian god of magic, reinforcing the legend that the cards were created in the initiation temples of the mysterious East. Their invention has also been attributed to the Order of the Knights Templar, an ascetic military Order founded in 1188 to protect pilgrims and guard the routes to the Holy Land.

Whatever the rumours about their appearance, the Tarot is closely linked with our modern deck of playing cards. It is generally accepted by scholars that the earliest playing cards originated in China and Korea, dating back at least to the 11th century.

If Tarot cards, as seems most likely, were devized originally somewhere in Northern Italy, it can be surmized that their makers were perhaps inspired by oriental cards

brought from the east by merchants returning to the great trading port of Venice. The original 78-card Tarot pack is generally referred to in Italy as the Venetian or Piedmontese Pack, to differentiate it from later offshoots.

A collection of Major Arcana cards from different periods, and in different designs.

Sixteenth century hand coloured engraving depicting people using a deck of cards. They are probably playing the game of Tarrochi.

Tarot Techniques

The basic idea in using the tarot is that the cards are shuffled and a 'spread' created. This means taking cards in sequence from the top of the shuffled pile and placing them in a particular pattern with the cards face up. The position of a card in the spread will signify a particular subject, such as the past or future of the person consulting the cards, the questioner or 'querent', and a specific card thus positioned will be interpreted according to its meaning.

You will see from this that, having posed a question to the Tarot deck which the querent requires to be answered, the cards chosen and placed in the spread appear simply by chance, as the pack is first shuffled. It is 'fate' or 'chance' which determines which card appears in which position.

Before making the spread, the cards are shuffled in such a way that some cards will appear upside down and others the right way up. A card that appears upside down, or 'reversed', has a different meaning than if it had appeared the right way.

Each card has a particular interpretation but it is not quite as straightforward as this, as the relationships that appear between different cards in a spread should be taken into account too.

How the Tarot is Structured

There are 78 cards in the deck, which is divided into two parts: the Major Arcana or Trumps, and the Minor Arcana. The word 'arcana' means mysteries or secrets. The Minor Arcana consists of 56 cards divided into four suits, each suit having ten Pip cards and four Court cards.

Apart from the extra Court card in each suit (the Knight), the Minor Arcana resembles a pack of modern playing cards, but the suits have different names: Wands, Rods or Batons (corresponding to Clubs); Cups (corresponding to Hearts); Swords (corresponding to Spades); and Coins, Pentacles or Discs (corresponding to Diamonds). Court cards are usually called King, Queen, Knight and Page.

The 22 cards of the Major Arcana form a sequence of 21 numbered cards, plus one unnumbered card called the Fool, which is sometimes numbered zero. Each of the Major Arcana cards depicts a strange scene which appears to have allegorical significance, telling a story or conveying a message. Each card is appropriately titled – the Sun, the Lovers, the Tower, the Hanged Man, Justice, the Emperor, the Star, the Chariot, to name a few.

There is a specific order to the Major Arcana cards, but you will notice that some decks deviate from this. The cards of Justice and Strength are most commonly transposed, this occurring, for example, in the popular Rider-Waite Tarot deck.

Cards from the Rider-Waite tarot deck.

The Major Arcana

It seems likely that the Tarot cards and in particular the Major Arcana were devized to represent grades or stages in a system of initiation. It is possible to interpret the meanings of the cards in terms of a sequence of events or lessons to be learnt. There seem to be close links with the system of alchemy whose devotees believed in the 'Hermetic' philosophy and underwent training leading to spiritual enlightenment.

These ancient doctrines have been examined afresh in modern times, particularly by C.G. Jung, who described the alchemists' work in terms of what he called 'psychic integration' or 'individuation'. The Major Arcana in this light becomes more than just a tool for divination but a way of learning about ones inner self and deeper motivations.

If we examine the 22 Tarot trumps with this in mind, we find that they fall naturally into two groups, with the Wheel of Fortune significantly at the midpoint. The turning point between one half of life and the other is of critical importance, sometimes precipitating a mid-life crisis. In this context the Wheel of Fortune represents the stage at which the peak is passed and the descent begins.

Set of Major Arcana cards from the Oswald Wirth deck.

The Minor Arcana: Cups and Batons

The Minor Arcana is divided into four suits: Batons (or Wands), Swords, Cups and Coins (or Pentacles). Each suit corresponds to one of the four astrological elements, Fire, Air, Water and Earth.

The suit of Cups corresponds to the element of Water. The Cup represents our ability to contain and to manage our feelings and emotions. Hence the suit of Cups is associated with feelings and emotions – the cup can be empty or full, it can be of great concern or ignored, its contents can be poison or elixir. The liquid contained by the cup symbolizes the sea of the unconscious, the source of all life, the most liquid, changeable formless and yet most powerful force in our world. As the Holy Grail, the cup can be a cornucopia, supplying all our wishes in a never-ending supply.

The suit of Batons corresponds to the element of Fire. Fire is a creative force which can illumine and warm, or, if uncontrolled, will burn up and destroy. Batons represent the creative urge, the imagination and the will to bring ones dreams into reality.

This suit has much to do with dominion and the establishing of power through strength, strife and victory. Its negative connotations being of oppression and the misuse of power.

The Minor Arcana: Coins and Swords

The suit of Coins corresponds to the element of Earth. Its realm is that of the material world, our possessions, our material successes and losses, whether we are prudent and thrifty or wasteful, whether we will have wealth or suffer poverty. This suit also represents earthly power and the ability to make practical changes in our lives.

The suit of Swords corresponds to the element of Air. It has much to do with the way we think, the things we believe to be true or not. It is also a very active suit often suggesting conflict and strife and the outcome of our battles to earn success. Sorrow and despair can be found in these cards as well as attainment and happiness.

Here is a summary of each card in the four suits:

Tarot reader in Romany costume consults the Tarot cards for her client sitting to her right.

Cups	Batons	Coins	Swords
1 Love	1 New beginnings	1 Prosperity	1 Triumph
2 Partnership	2 Strength	2 Movement	2 Friendship
3 Fruition	3 Dreams into reality	3 Establishment	3 Strife
4 Familiarity	4 Satisfaction	4 Stability	4 Respite
5 Reassessment	5 Obstacles	5 Material worries	5 Futility
6 Memories	6 Victory	6 Generosity	6 A battle won
7 Choice	7 Determination	7 Taking care	7 Foresight
8 Capitulation	8 Activity	8 Reward	8 End of adversity
9 Goodwill	9 Strength	9 Dormancy	9 Martyrdom
10 Love	10 A burden	10 Family security	10 Ruin

The Court Cards

In a Tarot reading, the Court cards are generally thought to represent particular individuals – either the querent, people known to the querent, or people he or she will meet.

The Court cards are part of the Minor Arcana and therefore are associated with the suits. The elements associated with the suits affect the personalities of the characters depicted. The Court cards in the suit of Batons are influenced by the element of Fire, which makes them lively and extroverted, while the Court cards in the suit of Cups are under the influence of the element of Water, which makes the characters they represent quiet, introverted and inclined to daydream.

The Court cards in the Air suit of Swords represent intellectual people who depend upon rational thinking, while the Court cards of the Earth suit of Coins are practical, common-sense people, good with their hands, skilled at making things work or at least with the potential to do so.

Links With Astrology

Apart from the association of the four suits with the four astrological elements, astrological symbolism abounds in the Tarot. Images such as the lion in the Strength card obviously correlate with the sign Leo; the Chariot with lunar crescents evokes the sign Cancer; similarly the lunar images of the High Priestess mark her as a goddess of the moon; the association of the Death card with the sign Scorpio is clear; the garden couch of the Empress is decorated with a Venus symbol, clearly evoking Venus; the Tower is destroyed by a burst of energy which is of the planet Mars; and the Sun card literally corresponds to the astrological symbolism of the sun.

These and many other associations have been made between the astrological symbols of the zodiac and the planets and the images found on the Tarot cards. This is useful in helping to bring new dimensions of meaning to the cards and also demonstrates quite ˙clearly that different systems of divination have much in common – when you learn about one system you are learning about the others too.

Getting Started

Having obtained your Tarot deck, my suggestion is to try a reading straight away, perhaps using the simple three-card spread which is described on page 72. There is nothing like learning by doing and no matter how much you learn the meanings of the individual cards you will find that the essence of the Tarot does not reveal itself until you actually use it in a reading.

Be quite clear about the question that you wish to ask. This is a general rule relevant to any divination system. A question whose meaning and motives are vague or ill-defined will result in an answer that is also unclear. However, this does not mean that you cannot ask general questions. For example, you, or the person for whom you are doing a reading, may simply wish to have a reading that summarizes your current situation and describes where exactly it is leading. You may be confused about some issue in your life, or uncertain about the correct decision to make. The Tarot will help to clarify your circumstances.

Another general piece of divination advice which can be applied to the Tarot is to resist asking the same question twice. This applies particularly if you don't like the answer that the reading gives. Also, the same question should not be asked within a short period of time, otherwise the answers will be conflicting and confusing. The rule is to wait until your circumstances have made a definite change before consulting the Tarot again on the same issue.

The Tarot cards associated with the zodiacal constellations. This shows the relationship between the signs Taurus to Pisces, in alternating order.

The Tarot Works

There is an aura of mystery surrounding the Tarot and it is this mystery that we will penetrate in the following chapter. Because the Tarot comes from a mystical tradition, it is treated with reverence and quite rightly so.

There are some, however, who mistakenly believe it to be a bad influence, holding superstitious fears about its effects and this problem will also be addressed, together with some answered questions about how the Tarot actually works. Although the results of a Tarot reading seem to depend on chance as the only factor to determine the cards which appear, there is more to it than that. Insights into how the Tarot works have been achieved in recent times and these provide us with the means to make the Tarot an effective system for revealing our own past, present and future.

towards enlightenment into the spiritual nature of the world in which we live.

In more modern times, this viewpoint has been brought up to date so that the Tarot can be regarded as a tool to use in giving insights about our inner self and can be used as a teaching aid in the process of self-development. These qualities of the Tarot will impinge on our exploration of its oracular properties and should be kept in mind as you read through the book. More of this later.

Two women consulting the Marseilles deck.

What It's For

The Tarot is an oracle, a means for divining the future. This is the main feature of the Tarot which we will be focusing on. The Tarot is more than this, for it not only gives insights into where we are heading in the future but it will also describe our situation in the past and in the present too. Divination is not just to do with the future, but includes all those aspects of our selves that we are unaware of, and this includes past and present too.

Although it is the use of the Tarot as an oracle that we will be dealing with, it is worth noting that its value extends beyond this. You will see how some of the cards seem to tell an unfolding story, particularly as we consider those in the Major Arcana. The story tells of different stages as we grow and develop in life, the sort of difficulties and tests that need to be met and dealt with and the means for solving our problems.

The Tarot cards were once thought of as depicting a series of initiations into the secrets of life and were used as a tool to teach what these experiences were all about. In particular, the Hermetic philosophy interpreted the cards as if they were a book explaining a route that could be taken

How It Works

The first thing to do is to be quite clear about the particular question that you want to put to the Tarot. This does not need to be a specific question but could be quite general, about your current situation, for example.

Having formulated your question, this should be held in your mind while the cards in the whole deck are thoroughly shuffled. When this has been done, the cards are placed in a pile face down. The cards are then taken in sequence from the top of the pile and placed, still face down, in a pattern or 'spread' chosen from the different options described in 'Making a Spread' page 70. Each card in the spread will be associated with some particular area of life, according to the spread chosen. For example, one card might represent the past, another the outcome, etc.

Then all of the cards are turned over so that they now lie face up. It is important that all of them are turned over before the reading begins so that they are not interpreted in isolation from one another, but the relationships between the meanings of the cards can be taken into account too. The final part of the process is to interpret the cards according to their specific meanings.

Syncronicity

So, how can the Tarot actually work? It seems impossible, given that the cards are shuffled so that the ones appearing in a reading do so in a completely random fashion, chosen only by the whims of chance. There is no denying that chance is the only factor involved, but what is its nature? A clue to this can be gained from the work of the psychologist, C.G. Jung. He defined two types of chance events.

The first type is what we commonly mean by chance, namely a purely random coincidence of events which occur in a meaningless fashion or pattern. It is the second type of chance event which is of significance in understanding how the Tarot works. This type of event Jung called 'syncronicity' to make it clear that chance events falling into this category have a special quality.

Syncronicity describes a chance coincidence which is imbued with meaning by the person, or persons, who experience it. In other words, the event has personal significance. This is exactly what happens when an oracle such as the Tarot is consulted.

Some people believe that the future is completely worked out and no matter what we do, particular events will come to pass.

It is difficult to describe syncronicity because it is an experience but the point is that even though the cards in a reading appear in a random fashion, their chance appearance is given significance by the person to whom the reading refers. The cards then take on a light and meaning of their own which relate specifically to the questioner who is having the reading.

Fate & Free Will

The next question to consider is, given that the Tarot indicates a particular outcome to a situation, is it inevitable that the events it predicts will happen? In other words, is the future preordained and fixed or do the choices we make in the present, affect what will happen in the future? This is partly a matter of belief. Some people believe that the future is completely worked out and no matter what we do, particular events will come to pass. There are others who say that the future is completely determined by the choices that we make in our lives.

My own opinion is that there is a balance point between these two views, that there are elements in life which are fated but that we have a certain amount of free will and choice too. The balance point can shift towards one direction or the other but always remains somewhere between the two. For example, the more aware we are of a situation, the more we are conscious of the different routes or choices that we can make. The more unaware or unconscious that we are, the less we are able to make any choices at all.

Because the Tarot is a tool for bringing awareness about our lives and the consequences of our actions, it should be seen as a means to bring more, not less, freedom to choose the future.

A Mirror of the Self

If you study different oracles, you will find that they all have much in common. In the Tarot, for example, there are strong links with astrology and also numerology, the oracle which uses number symbolism. The ancient Chinese oracle called the *I Ching* or 'Book of Changes' contains much of value too, particularly in its attitude to the future. The *I Ching* states that everything is in a state of flux, one thing is always changing into another, the present is always changing into the future.

The point is that if you can determine the changes that are going on in the present, you can go with this flow knowing what the future outcome will be and can even help to influence the direction, thus influencing the future. The Tarot should be regarded in this light too, showing how things are changing, for the better or worse. You can then be

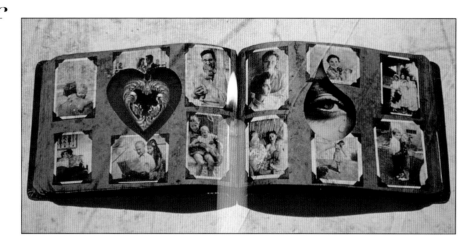

prepared for the future, looking at life not as a series of isolated events but as one great unfolding pattern where past and present have a direct relationship with the future.

This brings us to the idea that the Tarot mirrors the events of life. It does not determine them but simply reflects them. More than this it does not reflect the physical outer world, but shows us what is going on inside our selves. It is a mirror of the self.

You can then be prepared for the future, looking at life not as a series of isolated events but as one great unfolding pattern where past and present have a direct relationship with the future.

A Mirror for the Future

The idea of the Tarot as a mirror is an effective way of understanding what is going on when it is consulted. It is easy to see a refection of our physical natures in a glass mirror, but extremely difficult to get an objective view of what is going on in our lives, to see our 'selves'. To do this it would be necessary to step outside ourselves and look back to view from this new vantage point. This is precisely the opportunity that the Tarot affords us.

Regarding it as a mirror which reflects back all the possibilities for past, present, and future, which we already hold inside ourselves but of which we are unaware or simply have difficulty in seeing, turns the Tarot into a very effective and useful tool. Adopting this approach to it, asking can you

see yourself in this card, in this reading, also has the effect of taking out from the Tarot all the difficulties that some people have with it.

Adopting this view, if you see something bad in the Tarot, see something that you would rather not see, then this is in you and not in the cards – they are reflecting back what is already in yourself. So, if anyone tells you that the Tarot cards are a bad influence, point out that seeing a bad influence in the cards is a reflection of something that lies in the person, not in the cards. This approach does not take any of the magic out of the cards, does not reduce their ability to probe into the future, for they reflect what is to come about as well as what is happening right now.

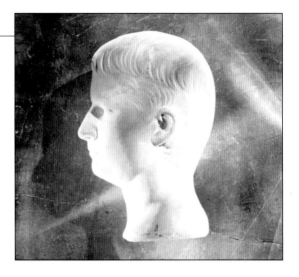

Tarot Images and the Unconscious

Let's take this understanding about how the Tarot works, a step further. We have seen how it will reflect what we are unaware of, what is going on in our unconscious selves. This gives a key to how it is possible to reflect the future as well as the present and the past.

The unconscious contains all our memories, it is a storehouse for our thoughts, feelings, ideas, images, daydreams, everything which we create inside ourselves. It is also the source of our dreams and fantasies. You will know from your dreams that the unconscious is not bound by the normal laws of everyday life. Seemingly impossible things can happen, and, interestingly, our dreams, and therefore the unconscious, are not bound by the constraints of time. It is not limited by the dimensional world in which we live our everyday lives. Although we are unable to move backwards or forwards in time but live in the ever present now, the unconscious seems to have no such constraint, as witnessed by our dreams whose reality can cross all of the dimensions of space and time.

The Tarot reflects what is going on in the unconscious, it can therefore reflect the future.

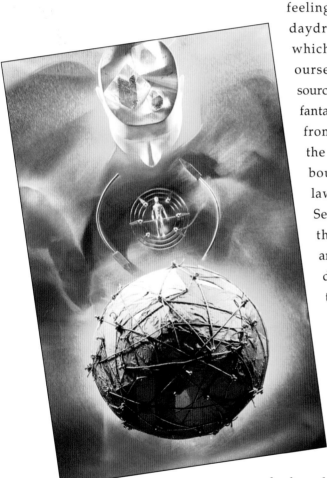

Tarot Archetypes

The unconscious contains what Jung called 'archetypes', or archetypal energies. These are the building blocks which form the foundation of our consciousness and our individual psyches. The archetypes are made known to us in many ways including through the images of mythology, religion and fairy tale. They are the gods, goddesses and phantoms of the land of storytelling. Rather than these gods and goddesses living 'out there', perhaps somewhere up Mount Olympus as the Ancient Greeks would have it, they live in us, in the unconscious.

These archetypes describe ways of behaving which are, to a certain extent, predictable. We can find out how they behave, what their individual personalities are like by reading about the ancient gods and goddesses of different cultures. Or we can find out by consulting the Tarot.

The Tarot cards clearly represent different archetypes. This is particularly obvious when you consider the Court cards and the cards in the Major Arcana. Perhaps less obvious are the archetypes represented by the Minor Arcana, for these depict situations. Nevertheless, they are all symbols, representations of the different archetypal energies which live in all of us and this is the reason why the Tarot is such an effective mirror for the unconscious.

Self-Development with the Tarot

Before returning again to the use of the Tarot as an oracle, consider first the use of the Tarot as a tool for self-development. It is of no benefit to know more about ourselves, more about what the future may hold in store, if we do nothing about it. The Tarot can help. One way, which I will describe in fuller detail in a later chapter, is to use the cards as objects for meditation.

When you have finished a reading, there is a temptation to return all the cards to the pack. Resist this and select one from the reading which seemed to have particular significance for you, or which spoke the loudest to you. Keep this card with you, or at least hold it in your memory for a little while to come.

The reason that this is a useful thing to do is that, because the cards represent archetypes and because they contain symbols – the language of the unconscious – the card that you choose will have an effect on you, on your unconscious, such that its meaning will unfold and become clearer with time.

A Tarot card can in this way become an aid to self-development, gradually revealing its meaning and stirring up thoughts, feelings and images from your unconscious which will give you a new view on life, helping you to grow inwardly and achieve insights about yourself and your needs.

Psychic Powers

Doing a Tarot reading involves two different facilities. The first is simply to be able to interpret the cards according to their meanings. You will find these explained in full in later chapters. The other facility is to give full reign to your intuition about the meaning of the cards.

A good reading can be produced simply by interpreting the cards according to the book, but a good reading can really come to life if you allow your imagination a little free reign, particularly seeing the connections that exist between different cards in a spread.

Allow your imagination to rise up in response to what you see in the cards and don't be afraid to overlay the textbook interpretations with your own imaginative insights. You will find that, if you allow this process to happen, the cards will begin to speak to you so that you can almost forget the particular meanings of the cards and simply rely on the promptings from your own unconscious. For me, this is the best sort of reading, but it cannot be done effectively without first learning the significance of each card, even if you then abandon these meanings to a lesser or greater degree.

Developing this process is akin to developing psychic powers, for your insights, coming in response to the cards, then come from inside yourself, from the wellspring of your unconscious.

A good reading can really come to life if you allow your imagination a little free reign.

Building Blocks of the Tarot

XII The Hang   II The   XVI   Ten of P   Six of F   King of P   Thr   Queen of   Eigh   Three   Nine o   Ten of Wands

The whole of the Tarot pack is built on the idea of groups of cards and the relationships between them.

When the cards in a reading are interpreted, they are not treated in isolation, but the relationships between them are considered as having equal importance with what the individual cards mean. Indeed, the whole of the Tarot pack is built on the idea of groups of cards and the relationships between them.

In this chapter we will consider what these groups or 'building blocks' are. This will help you to learn about the cards, as it is easier to remember what they are all about if you can slot them into a particular category. Also, it gives an impression of the cohesive nature of the Tarot pack and the depth of meaning that it contains. In particular we will consider the number symbolism associated with each card and this will show how there are links between cards of the same number in each suit.

An Overview

As a resumé of what we have learnt so far, refer back to page 8. When we consider the structure of the 78 cards, they will be divided into different sections, Major Arcana, Minor Arcana, Court cards and the numbered suits. Remember though that when preparing a reading, the pack of cards is treated as a whole. All the different sections are shuffled together so that when the cards in a reading are peeled from the top, there is an equal chance of cards appearing from anywhere in the complete pack.

Generally speaking, the Major Arcana cards are more powerful in influence than those in the Minor Arcana, hence the differentiation of Major and Minor. This does not mean that they are necessarily more important, although they could be. However, the forces that they represent are fundamental ones and therefore are interpreted as having a powerful influence.

The Court cards are usually interpreted as representing particular people who the questioner will know or come to know. These are people who are influencing the situation that is being considered and the Court cards describe their personalities and the likely way that they will behave towards the querent. A Court card might even represent the questioner themselves.

Numerology and the Tarot

Numerology is the study of number symbolism and its use in divination. It can be treated as an oracle in itself. Because the Tarot pack is not randomly created, having definite patterns of relationship between the cards and between different sections of the pack, the patterns that exist can be explored in terms of number symbolism. For example, all of the Minor Arcana cards having the same number of 'pips' will have something in common. What they have in common is described by the number associated with this card.

Numerologically speaking, each number has a particular character and meaning, representing certain energies or creative forces. The number sequence from 1 to 10 has a pattern of development with the number 1 representing beginnings, the number 6, midway through the cycle, suggesting fulfilment, and the end number, 10, in the cycle having the quality of completion. So, as you begin to look at the meanings of the cards in the Minor Arcana it is useful first to compare the cards in each suit which carry the same number, and also to think about where they lie in the sequence or cycle of numbers from 1 to 10.

Numerologically speaking, each number has a particular character and meaning, representing certain energies or creative forces.

Number Symbolism

When you read the meanings of the cards in the Minor Arcana you will find that each one is headed with a keyword describing its number symbolism. The association with the card meaning might not be directly obvious but nevertheless the number symbolism should be taken into account when interpreting the card.

For example, although the number 5 represents creative forces, the five card often depicts a situation of stress and turmoil. This simply means that a difficult situation is not necessarily lacking in a creative aspect. The number symbolism adds an important facet to the interpretation of the cards.

I have only mentioned the Minor Arcana with respect to number symbolism but the Major Arcana and the Court cards can be considered in this light too.

Here is a summary of the meaning of the numbers from 1 to 10, these meanings being found at the heading to the descriptions of each Minor Arcana card.

1	Birth	6	Insight
2	Polarity	7	Contemplation, inner work
3	Resolution	8	Totality
4	Healing	9	Completion
5	Creativity	10	Conclusion

You will find that the first five cards in each of the suits suggest the movement from a beginning towards a goal, whereas the remaining cards suggest turning into the final straight and moves towards home again.

The Major Arcana

The Major Arcana cards, numbered from 0 to 21 represent degrees of initiation or simply the different experiences that are common to us as we go through life. They represent stages, or signposts along the way.

Try laying the 21 cards out in a figure of eight pattern as shown in the illustration so that the two cards at the crossing point are number 10, the Wheel of Fortune, and number 21 the World.

The cards in the top half of the figure, cards 0 to 10, represent the first half of life. They are more worldly, concerned with making ones way in life and making a mark on the world. They tend to be extrovert cards to do with doing, achieving, seeking and gaining power and so on.

The cards in the bottom half of the figure, cards 11 to 21, represent the second half of life. They are more inward looking, concerned with the meaning of life, the greater pattern, spiritual values and goals. They tend to be

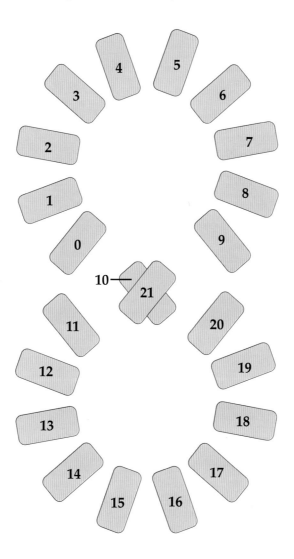

introverted cards to do with gaining insight into the inner worlds, coming to terms with and dealing with psychological forces.

The two cards which fall at the centre of the figure, 10 and 11, represent the end of the first half of life and the beginning of the second.

The Minor Arcana

Strictly speaking, the Court Cards are part of the Minor Arcana, but we will consider them separately. The numbered Minor Arcana cards are divided into the four suits containing ten cards in each. Each card is given a specific meaning, and the essential pattern of the suit is described by the number symbolism explained above. In other words, the 'one' cards represent beginnings and the 'ten' cards – completion.

It is worth noting the influence on the meanings of the cards that were given to the A.E. Waite pack published in 1910. These were based on the teachings of the magical order of the Golden Dawn which had attributed to the minor cards symbolism taken from the Qabalists' Tree of Life. The reason for mentioning this is that although the Tarot cards have been in use for many centuries, the meanings attributed to the Minor Arcana cards in particular, in the majority of packs available today, are heavily influenced by the Golden Dawn and the Waite pack. The attributions of the cards can therefore be traced back to a system which was devized at the end of the 19th century. It is this system which has been adopted and adapted in the interpretations which follow in later chapters.

The meanings of the cards are continuously developing with time so that although the Tarot has strong roots, it is an ever-growing system of enlightenment, changing and adapting to suit modern times.

The Court Cards

The Court Cards consist of King, Queen, Knight and Page (or Knave) in each suit. These were radically altered in the system attributed to the Golden Dawn but we will stick with their more traditional meanings and roles. Remember that the court cards represent actual people in a reading rather than situations. The type of person and the influence that they have will depend on where they fall in a spread and also the interpretation given to each card.

Their characters depend partly on which suit they fall in. This will be considered in the next section. Their characters also depend on their status – whether King, Queen, Knight or Page.

The **Kings** are depicted as masculine, powerful people tending to be leaders and initiators. They like to be served and can be fearful enemies if crossed.

The **Queens** are also powerful but have a greater sensitivity towards the inner nature of people and are more subtle in the way that they act.

The **Knights** make excellent allies as they are competent, skillful and willing characters.

The **Pages** are youthful and lacking in worldly experience. They are willing to learn, can be enthusiastic and need to be told what to do.

The meanings of the cards are continuously developing with time so that although the Tarot has strong roots, it is an ever-growing system of enlightenment, changing and adapting to suit modern times.

One of the most useful correspondences between the Tarot cards and other systems of divination is the relationship of the four suits with the four elements of astrology: Air, Earth, Water and Fire.

The Four Suits

The Minor Arcana is divided into four suits. Their properties are as follows.

The suit of **Swords** is the suit of activity, movement and conflict. Swords seek progress by making changes and then establishing a new order ruled by the law. Swords are divisive and can cause conflict between two parties, polarizing people into different camps. Swords stir things up.

The suit of **Coins** is the suit of material affairs. Money matters and material security, the amassing (or losing) of wealth and the power which wealth brings are all under the aegis of the Coins. Stability and security and the degree of material comfort are also the concern of this suit.

The suit of **Cups** is the suit of matters of the heart. Emotional concerns, relationships, shifting feelings and their manipulation are all within the compass of the Cups. Love, partnership and emotional ties figure prominently here.

The suit of **Batons** is the suit of creative activity and the power of the will. Batons work in the field of inspiration and the imagination bringing new ways of looking at the world, making progress through invention and dynamic change. Batons see the potential and possibilities in a situation and can act accordingly.

The Four Elements

One of the most useful correspondences between the Tarot cards and other systems of divination is the relationship of the four suits with the four elements of astrology: Air, Earth, Water and Fire.

The Swords correspond with Air; Coins correspond with Earth; Cups correspond with Water; Batons correspond with Fire. The meanings of the four elements give further insights into the significance of the cards in each of the suits.

Air and Earth

Each sign of the zodiac is associated with one of the four elements. Gemini, Libra and Aquarius are the Air signs.

Air is the element which rules all matters of the mind, of rational thinking. Air is thoughtful, showing lively interest in all subjects, is a good teacher, talker and communicator. The Air element is masculine, extroverted and outgoing. Its positive attributes are the ability to gain insight and think things through. Negatively expressed, it is argumentative and dogmatic.

Taurus, Virgo and Capricorn are the Earth signs of the zodiac.

Earth is practical and resourceful, liking to put down firm roots. It enjoys increase and the process of gaining material possessions and wealth, being at home in the world of business and commerce. Earth is constructive and skilled in practical matters and is comfortable in the physical world, liking technology and crafts. Earth enjoys the good things in life, good food, clothes and entertainment. Earth is feminine, introverted and receptive. Its positive attributes are reliability and the ability to make things work. Negatively expressed, it is wasteful, and boorish.

Water and Fire

Cancer, Scorpio and Pisces are the Water signs of the zodiac.

Water is the experience of emotions and feelings. It is changeable, unpredictable and adaptable, being easily hurt and easily persuaded. Water is protective and nurturing, compassionate and caring. Its ability to protect can make it quite tenacious and a forceful opponent. Water can have a sense of charisma and power, or can be a dreamer and highly artistic. Water is feminine, introverted and receptive. Its positive attributes are sensitivity to the needs of others and the ability to adapt to changing situations. Negatively expressed, it is manipulative and self-centred.

Aries, Leo and Sagittarius are the Fire signs of the zodiac.

Fire is creative and intuitive with a penchant for action and activity. Always ready to confront a situation head on, Fire is

dynamic and full of energy. It is theatrical as well as forceful, a go-getter. Fire likes to initiate projects and be in command, it is also prone to deep thought and sees itself as a great teacher. Fire is masculine, extroverted and outgoing. Its positive attributes are the ability to make things happen and to see new possibilities. Negatively expressed, it is highly destructive and wanton, having no regard for damage caused in getting its own way.

Fire is creative and intuitive with a penchant for action and activity.

The Four Grail Hallows

Before leaving this chapter, it is worth noting how the symbolism of the four suits has prominence in other traditions, other than the Tarot. In alchemy and numerology the number four has significance as the number of healing and wholeness, containing four opposing yet complementary elements. Even the geography of our physical world is 'ruled' by the number four, being divided into the four points of the compass.

In the stories of the Holy Grail, four sacred objects are spoken of, the 'Grail Hallows', and their association with the four Tarot suits is clear.

The first hallow is the Grail cup itself, which corresponds with the suit of Cups.

The second hallow is the 'Sword of the Spirit', a legendary sword, wielded by King David in the Old Testament, whose significance can probably be associated with the mythical Excalibur. The correspondence is with the suit of Swords.

The third hallow is the lance, said to be the lance which pierced Christ's side as he hung on the cross. Its correspondence is with the suit of Batons or Staves.

The fourth hallow is the platter from which Christ and his disciples eat the Paschal Lamb. Its correspondence is with the suit of Coins, or Discs.

In the Tarot is found a strange combination of pagan images, with hints from the Christian tradition too, as described by the symbols found in the Grail stories.

Past, Present and Future

By now you should have an overall picture of what the Tarot is all about, how it is used and what its purpose is. Throughout this book, an emphasis is placed on the idea of relationships in the Tarot, not only between the cards in the deck but also between the reader and the questioner and between past, present and future.

In the previous chapter, we examined the card relationships and the structure of the Tarot and now we can turn to some of the wider issues and relationships that provide insight into how the Tarot works and how it is interpreted. This will complete the first part of the book before considering what the individual cards represent.

The Hermetic Art

The Tarot cards are a system of alchemy, in other words they have the ability to transform a situation. The individual cards are like psychological chemicals which when combined in a certain way, produce new compounds with different properties to the original constituents. Which chemicals are chosen for combining depends on which cards are drawn in a reading.

The old alchemists were on the trail of the substance that would turn their chemicals into gold, and this is the general view of what alchemy was all about. But many of the alchemists, who believed in the 'Hermetic Philosophy' thought of alchemy as much more than this. They believed that their experiments did not only involve their chemicals but that they too were part of the experiment – how it turned out depended just as much on their attitude to it as what chemicals were used.

This is exactly like a Tarot reading. When you prepare a spread in response to a question being asked of the cards, you are conducting an alchemical experiment, one whose outcome depends on the cards *and* you and the questioner. There is a psychological process at work here which involves putting these three things together to create a particular 'chemistry'.

Because the result of the experiment does not depend solely on the cards chosen, but involves the reader and querent too, it means that no two readings will be exactly the same, even if the same cards were chosen. Your attitude and mood will have changed. Each moment in time has its own particular characteristics and this affects the outcome too, so that exactly when the reading is conducted has its influence on the results.

Timing

The alchemists considered that the exact time when they conducted their experiments was important for obtaining successful results. If the experiment was conducted at the right time then it would work, if not, then it would fail. They were therefore interested in astrology as this would reveal favourable timings from the position of the planets, particularly as each of the planets was said to correspond with the metals which the alchemists used.

I am not saying that you need to cast a horoscope each time you do a Tarot reading, but am suggesting that you consider the timing of your readings. Being aware of this factor will help you to understand why a reading may be successful or otherwise. Before you prepare a reading, it is worth asking the querent why they chose to ask their particular question at this time, or what circumstances have made them feel that now is the moment that they have felt compelled to consult the Tarot.

In reading the cards, be aware of all the different linking factors that are involved. For example, the questioner may seem to be only concerned about what is going to happen in the future, but remember that what will happen has a specific relationship with events in the present and the past. The future can only be understood in terms of these connections.

The alchemists considered that the exact time when they conducted their experiments was important for obtaining successful results.

Card Psychology

Some people credit the Tarot cards with having some sort of mystical property in their ability to foretell the future. This is not so. All the cards consist of is a series of images and symbols, nothing more and nothing less. The reason why these images and symbols seem to have the ability to answer the questions put to them is because of the involvement of the reader and the questioner. There is some psychological chemistry at work here and it is helpful in learning about how the cards work to understand a little of what this psychology is all about.

The World and Judgement cards from the nineteenth century Italian Tarocchi deck.

When you consult the Tarot, or when the querent asks his or her question, you already know the answer but it is unconscious. You are unaware of its existence. Modern psychology has discovered a process called 'projection' whereby contents of the unconscious mind are projected into the outside world where they can be observed as something separate from the person who projected them. This can happen, for example, in our relationships when we see qualities in people which really don't exist in them but which are in ourselves but on an unconscious level.

The point is that this projection process is at work when reading the Tarot. The cards act as a hook for unconscious projections. They capture the answers and then reflect them back in a manner which seems to be the cards telling us, but what is really happening is that the cards act as a mirror for answers that were in the unconscious just waiting to be drawn out.

The Holistic Universe

The great psychic Edgar Cayce believed in what he called the 'Akashic Record' which contained all the knowledge of the universe. He believed that it was possible with appropriate training, for the mind to be put in contact with this record and have access to information about the past, present and the future.

The Akashic Record has similarities with psychology's conception of the unconscious mind which is not bound by the normal laws of time and dimension. For example, our dreams, which are letters from the unconscious, seem to have no limitations imposed on them with regard to our everyday dimensional world.

We are 'holistic' beings having both a conscious and an unconscious mind. We live in an holistic universe where everything is connected including past, present and future. The Tarot simply mirrors this picture. So, when preparing a reading, don't be too surprised by all the connections and coincidences that you find are revealed by the cards, but when you do find them, encourage them and look for further connections. Creating a whole picture is the key to a successful reading. Remember that you won't be able to say anything new to the questioner, nothing that they don't know already even though unconsciously. But you will be able to show how the Tarot reveals new connections between events, people, places and so on. This is the alchemy of the Tarot at work.

Preparing for a Reading

We will cover the practicalities of shuffling the cards and laying them out in a spread in a later chapter, but there are some considerations here which will help to create a successful reading. Pay attention to details and try to get everything right. This includes

the environment that you use for your reading. The atmosphere should be peaceful and unlikely to be interrupted. The lighting should not be too bright and you can create an appropriate setting by burning some incense or an essential oil.

What you are aiming for is to encourage the Tarot images to capture the projections from your unconscious mind, and this won't work in an atmosphere that is not conducive to a meditative feel. Also, creating the right atmosphere helps to get the questioner involved too, helping them to take seriously the results that the Tarot cards will provide.

Become aware of all the factors that are likely to affect your reading, your and the questioner's mood and attitude, for example. The cards will only reveal to you what they see in you, so that a frivolous approach will only produce frivolous answers!

Left: Pay attention to details and try to get everything right.

The Temperance and Devil cards from the Marseilles deck (Tarocco di Marsiglia) designed in Geneva and printed in Milan 1804.

Reversed Cards

You will find in the next chapter that, with each interpretation of the meanings of the cards, there is a 'reversed' meaning. The cards are shuffled in such a way that some of the cards will be positioned upside-down in the spread. This is significant and has to be taken into account. The interpretations given of the reversed cards are shorter than those for the upright positions but this does not mean they are less significant or important. The reason for this is that the reversed meaning is directly related to that for its upright position, so that by knowing what this is you will have a pretty good idea of how to interpret the reversed card.

The reversed position tends to bring out the worst in a card so that, in general, a reversal shows a negative influence. You will

find that there are one or two exceptions to this rule. Also, how negative the influence is will depend on other cards in the reading and how the reversed card relates to them. For example, the overall tenor of a reading might be for success and achievement while a reversed card, rather than suggesting doom and gloom might simply be a restraining influence, keeping the querent's feet on the ground.

The reason for mentioning the reversed cards here is that, once again, their meaning depends partly on their relationship with the other cards in a reading.

Tarot Card Relationships

What is meant by the relationships between the cards is best shown by doing a reading. You will be surprised at how common themes crop up between the cards, how appropriate they are, and how they may show a progression from events that have taken place in the past to those which are likely to occur in the future.

It is sometimes suggested that the cards are placed face down and only turned over when they are considered for interpretation. There is much to recommend placing them all face up to start with because then you can immediately become aware of the pattern of cards which have cropped up, where the coincidences lie and where the emphasis is being placed by the cards.

Indeed, you will discover that it is common for all of the cards to point to a single theme or solution to the querent's question. When this happens you will know that the reading is working. It is only when the cards seem to be isolated from one another that you know you have problems.

When doing a reading, I suggest that first you consider the cards as a whole, then interpret them individually, and then, at the end, come back to looking at them as a whole again, pointing out the common themes and the recurring insights that the cards provide.

Tarot Card Symbols

Now let's go to the opposite extreme and consider for a moment not the meanings of the individual cards but those of the symbols and images that are found on the cards. Some of them can be found on more than one card.

Various cards from a variety of different Tarot decks, showing symbols in both ancient and modern designs.

Pairs of columns symbolize the physical world and its vested authorities.

Stars and canopies symbolize the higher worlds available through increased awareness.

The throne is dominion, power, strength and fixity.

The pyramid is transmutation to reach a higher reality.

The square and triangle are the same in interpretation to the numbers four and three (see page 20).

The sphere represents completion and wholeness.

Towers symbolize strength and protection.

The crown symbolizes high status.

The sceptre symbolizes fertility.

Keys are responsibility and the means for unlocking a problem.

An arrow represents the strength of willpower.

A snake suggests wisdom.

Corn is a symbol for renewal and harvest.

Roses symbolize love.

Trees symbolize strength, union and the linking of heaven and earth.

The dog is loyalty, instinct and faithfulness.

Cats suggest intuition and perception.

Mountains symbolize a quest and the scaling of great heights.

A barren landscape represents lack of love and affection.

There are, of course, many other symbols to be found on the cards. The point here is that it is worth not only learning about the meaning of the cards, but also about the individual symbols which are included in each illustration.

How to Interpret

The first thing that you will need to do is to learn the meanings of the cards. This is not such a daunting task as you might imagine. Because of the way the cards are structured, the number symbolism, groupings of the cards and the pattern as you go through the Major and Minor Arcanas, you will find that these are all aids for your memory. For example, if you know what the overall meaning of the suit of Cups is, then you know something that all the cards in this suit have in common.

Even before you know what all the cards mean, start practising your readings. In fact, there is no reason why you should not do this straight away. In doing a reading, you will need to look up the meanings of the cards and this will be a great help in the learning process. Try to combine a systematic approach with learning by experience.

It is just as valuable to give some free reign to your imagination so that, if you feel a

card is suggesting a particular meaning but this is not included in the textbook interpretation, then go with your intuition. Have the confidence to do this. Later we will consider in more detail the role of imagination and intuition, because they make an important contribution to the interpretation process.

The Cards Cannot Lie

Keeping in mind that what you see in the cards is a reflection of what lies in the unconscious mind, or in the Akashic Record, if you prefer, then it is important to recognize that the cards cannot lie, in just the same way that a mirror cannot lie about what it reflects – what it shows depends on the light falling on it. Your skill as a Tarot reader corresponds with how well you can create this mirror, how clearly it will reflect the unconscious.

. . . the cards cannot lie, in just the same way that a mirror cannot lie about what it reflects . . .

The Tarot can only reflect the truth, what is there, so if what you discover seems obscure at first, don't reject it but try to clarify it. It is a general rule to accept what the Tarot says to you first and not to look for another meaning. So, especially if you don't like what you see, which will make acceptance harder, it is necessary to be completely open to the meaning of the cards.

There may be a reason for obscurity and, if the cards are distinctly negative, then remember that life is never perfect. It is not often that someone will consult the Tarot unless there is some sort of problem or difficulty in life which it is desired to solve. The cards will reflect this difficulty as well as point to where the solution might be.

And now we can turn to the meanings of the cards themselves.

The Major Arcana

In the next three chapters you will find interpretations of all of the Tarot cards. In this chapter we will cover the Major Arcana, in the next chapter the Court cards, and finally the Minor Arcana. The descriptions are given in such a way that you can make practical use of them in a Tarot reading straight away.

Until you are familiar with your cards and can interpret them without referring to their meaning, it is quite acceptable to look up the individual meanings and use them directly in your interpretation. Because this book is not geared to any specific Tarot pack, you can use the interpretations with any deck. When you get used to your own Tarot cards, you will be able to add depth to your interpretation by translating the particular images and symbols found on them.

0 The Fool

This card is sometimes unnumbered. The Fool represents a childlike quality, suggesting immaturity and lack of discipline. When the Fool appears in a spread it indicates new directions taken, acting on instinct rather than thinking things through. Like a child, the impulse is to act without considering or appreciating the consequences. 'Fools rush in where angels fear to tread', is an apt description of the situation here.

The Fool is innocent of his actions, not realizing the affect that they have on other people. His success comes from acting on instinct and whim so that actions can be carried out successfully which, if thought about, would never have been ventured in the first place.

Reversed Meaning

When reversed, the childlike quality of the Fool turns to childishness and impulsive behaviour becomes rash, over-risky, and wilful with no consideration of the negative effects that his actions have on others. Violent outbursts or tantrums are indicated.

This book is not geared to any specific Tarot pack and you can use the interpretations with any deck. In the following chapters (pages 31-69), we have used the 1JJ Swiss Tarot Pack © U.S. Games Systems, Inc., to illustrate the individual cards in the deck.

I The Magician or Juggler

LE MAT.

The Magician brings the qualities of great skill and dexterity to a situation. This is backed up by self-confidence and willpower, so that the Magician is quite a powerful, influential figure. His skill and dexterity can involve sleight of hand and an ability to manipulate circumstances to his own ends as if by magic. He also has the ability to adapt easily and to make something out of nothing.

The Magician shows the taking of initiative and the ability to make connections. He is a messenger, a mediator and a communicator. If maturity is also indicated, he becomes a wise sage, but without this, he is simply a fast talker, a spiv.

Reversed Meaning

Because the Magician is skillful and dexterous, when expressed negatively he becomes a deceiver and trickster, who is capable of manipulation for selfish ends. In this guise he will take what he needs, even resorting to theft. If the Magician appears reversed, look for underhand deceit and manipulation.

LE BATELEUR

II *The High Priestess*

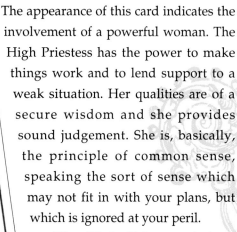

The appearance of this card indicates the involvement of a powerful woman. The High Priestess has the power to make things work and to lend support to a weak situation. Her qualities are of a secure wisdom and she provides sound judgement. She is, basically, the principle of common sense, speaking the sort of sense which may not fit in with your plans, but which is ignored at your peril.

The High Priestess brings healing to a situation, a healing based on natural forces. Her appearance in a reading indicates that natural forces are at work and that it is best to let them run their course. She may have an affinity with the healing arts, magic and spiritual mystery, but the results of her appearance are practical. She knows just what to do!

Reversed Meaning

In this position, the High Priestess simply doesn't know what she is talking about. She comes out with all sorts of advice, facts, beliefs, dogma and irrefutable statements, none of which have any basis in reality. It's all just mumbo jumbo.

III *The Empress*

The key to the meaning of the Empress is fertility, the ability to produce and make things grow. Her appearance suggests the importance of family matters, perhaps involving children and in particular the influence of the mother or a mother figure. She brings fruitfulness, progress and development. Under her influence there is a secure home base present which can give strong support to all undertakings.

The Empress provides support and protection, and in return demands faithfulness. If this is missing, or if she is betrayed then her anger and vengeance are indicated. She makes a powerful partner in marriage with a liking for domestic bliss and tradition. Her purpose is to create, to produce and then to support her creations.

Reversed Meaning

The Empress can be a stifling influence, overbearing, overprotective, not allowing growth and development to take place. Reversed she is a limiting, stultifying, overbearing influence. Obsessive jealousy is indicated and also a snobbery which is misplaced and causes repulsion and rejection. When she appears reversed, look for a child who is tied to mother's apron strings.

IV *The Emperor*

Whereas the Empress represents emotional power and strength, the Emperor is the bringer of worldly power – material success and wealth, seeking to establish his authority and to maintain the *status quo*. To do this he brings an indomitable spirit, powers of endurance and strong convictions.

When the Emperor appears, success in the material world is indicated particularly through the career or in business. He is a patriarch, a father figure who will punish if his laws are broken. He builds the structures within which to operate and provided you do not go outside this domain, there are rich rewards to be had. His is a life of action in the world, in business, in politics, his influence coming from the father or a father figure.

Reversed Meaning

Quite simply, the reversed meaning is the misuse of power, in a word, tyranny. The reversed Emperor is the over-domineering male who expresses dogma backed up with a rule by force. He is then an overblown personality full of his own importance and disliked for it.

V *The Pope or Hierophant*

This is the great upholder of tradition, particularly through religious values and morality – 'Thou shalt not . . .' His appearance brings the necessity to stick with the tried and tested, indicating that change or innovation is inappropriate.

The Hierophant has the ability to hold people together through a common set of rules to live by and a common belief in the nature of reality. He asks that you pay homage to this with obedience. In return he offers mercy, kindness, good advice and an alliance. He suggests that if you join his club you will have the support of all its members. If you go it alone, then you will be alone.

A representative of the old-school-tie network, the Hierophant's authority seems to be of a spiritual, abstract nature, rather than based in material power like the Emperor.

Reversed Meaning

Reversed, the Hierophant will catch you in unnecessary dogma, and meaningless ritual. Here, the suggestion is that outworn patterns of belief or activity are being perpetuated, preventing any further progress. Brain-washing and lack of the ability to think for oneself are indicated.

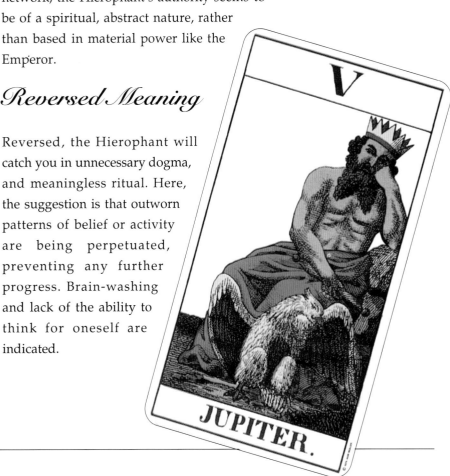

VI The Lovers

This is the card of the love affair, usually between two people, sometimes between a person and an object of passion. The result is attraction, flirtation, consummation. The Lovers bring the ability to see the world in a new light where all seems wonderful and new. An affair is indicated with the attendant experiences of pursuit and courtship, bringing the joys of youth and bright eyes to those involved. A new partnership is 'on the cards' and the discovery of a new and abiding love.

This card brings harmony and unanimity with the end result of a marriage and honeymoon period. It represents the uniting of opposites and the establishment of peace after a period of conflict.

Reversed Meaning

Blind or foolish action is the result of the Lovers caught in this position. Ones actions and judgement are clouded by an unrealistic attraction. There is a failure to see the bad in a situation, which is covered up with a superficial veneer. There may be unrequited love.

VII The Chariot

When the Chariot appears, there is a battle going on and if upright, the result is victory. The Chariot brings the usurping of the old order and the crowning of the new. It is an inevitable force for change and once on its way is unstoppable. The new order comes about through the defeat of an adversary and although the result is victory, the cost of this has to be taken into account. There may be some cleaning up to do after the event.

With victory comes responsibility to act in the proper fashion and to bring the vanquished into the fold. Wounds need healing as quickly and as effectively as possible, otherwise they may fester away beneath the surface only to open up again at a later date.

Reversed Meaning

Conquest is again indicated, but this time in defeat rather than victory. The reversed Chariot brings troubles and difficulties which have a momentum building up and which are difficult to stop. Beware of bullying and sabre-rattling which will surely lead to a setback and defeat.

VIII *Justice*

It does not always happen, but when this card appears, the rule of reason and the vanquishing of the unjust are the order of the day. Justice is done. Justice brings the correct balancing of power, neither too strong nor too weak, neither too much with one person nor with the other. The result of balancing power is justice and this in turn means the punishing of those in the wrong and the vindication of those in the right.

Well-meaning actions are afoot here and any advice which is given is good advice – take it! Together with fortitude and temperance, justice is one of three cardinal virtues offered by the Tarot, so the appearance of this card results in a reordering of the situation to create a 'rightful order'.

Reversed Meaning

In this position there may simply be a delay in the carriage of justice, or, at worst, it may be a 'miscarriage. Other indications in the spread will indicate which of these is the case. If a miscarriage has taken place in the past, then new light will be thrown on current circumstances. If it is to take place in the future, then best to prepare for the eventuality.

IX *The Hermit*

The Hermit asks that you step back from a situation, that you leave it alone and withdraw, at least for a while. Only by doing this can you create the necessary detachment so that things can be thought through clearly and objectively. The Hermit means that being cautious and prudent are appropriate to circumstances and that becoming hidden will bring advantages.

A period of solitude is called for and the Hermit will provide the space and the time for this retreat from the world. The time should be used for introspection so that ones true motives can be determined. The Hermit is turning away from the world, for a time only, so that batteries can be recharged and time given to oneself and ones own needs. Ignoring this call can lead to a deteriorating situation and even ill health.

Reversed Meaning

Reversed, the Hermit indicates futility and barrenness. He even brings desertion and the inability to face up to a situation. An ostrich with its head buried in the sand would sum up this situation. The Hermit now brings loneliness and a cynical attitude to life.

X Chance or the Wheel of Fortune

This card indicates the arrival of circumstances which offer good fortune. However, when the opportunity arises it must be seized otherwise it will pass and be lost. An important coincidence is indicated such that when the two events collide they create a set of unexpected but welcome circumstances.

Chance is a fickle thing and rarely does the same set of fortuitous circumstances arise twice. There is a hint here that no matter how carefully plans are laid, the unexpected cannot be accounted for. Indeed, room for the unexpected should be left, for fixity and rigidity can result in the fortunes of chance being denied entry. This is the card of 'syncronicity' which means that chance events will have great meaning and significance for you.

Reversed Meaning

The Wheel of Fortune now brings inauspicious omens and a foreboding atmosphere. Lost opportunities are in the air and the Wheel is running in contrary motion. When this card is reversed, decision making is best delayed and unnecessary risks avoided.

XI Strength

A testing of ones strength, bravery and fortitude is called for here, the card indicating that all these are available in quantity. When faced with a difficult or even seemingly impossible task, the appearance of Strength brings with it the ability to surmount the difficulties, to achieve the impossible.

Moral courage is the basis for physical strength and the ability to see things through. One of the most difficult tasks is to overcome ones instincts when this is the right thing to do, perhaps involving selfless behaviour or self-sacrifice of some kind. This is precisely what is needed when the Strength card crops up.

However, moral courage may be insufficient if the body is weak, so Strength should be accompanied by healthy exercise and diet if it is not to be undermined.

Reversed Meaning

Weakness is the result of Strength reversed, foolhardiness at best, cowardice at worst. Strength can here represent all brawn and no brain at work. Wasted effort may be indicated, for example, taking a sledge hammer to crack a nut, the result being the destruction of the nut.

XII *The Hanged Man*

A sacrifice is required here in order to obtain ones goal. The Hanged Man's viewpoint is upside down suggesting that lateral thinking is required. A completely different view of a situation is necessary before it will become clear. Giving something up in order to gain is the type of thinking required – less means more, loss means gain, failure means success, etc.

There is an element of surrender in this card, for the Hanged Man is helpless, is caught in a position from which it will be difficult to escape without help. The only thing he can do is give in to his position and abandon thoughts of all else. The result will be transition from one set of circumstances to another, and his appearance in a reading often points to this. The old must be abandoned before the new will be gained. The process will be an uncomfortable one, but the sacrifice must be made if progress is to be made. A key word is 'suspension'.

Reversed Meaning

Any confinement or 'suspension' is now self-inflicted and therefore the reversed Hanged Man means that punishment and pain is of ones own doing. There exists the possibility of release from the bondage of a situation.

XIII *Death*

A highly emotive card, Death indicates an end and a new beginning. In its upright position, the emphasis is on endings, completion of a project or phase. This card represents the cutting away of dead wood, or loss of outworn, unnecessary baggage. The changes suggested here are drastic and complete, with no gradual transformation but a sudden one. Like death, the boundary between the old and new situation is sharp and uncompromising. This does not mean that Death cannot be seen coming, although it may take one by surprise. When the event comes, it happens in the twinkling of an eye.

Death can also be interpreted as great loss, failure and illness, if other cards in the reading support this negative viewpoint.

Reversed Meaning

The Death card now suggests that a disaster has been, or can be, avoided. There is also the meaning that an awakening is taking place, the dawning of an important realization, and the emphasis is now on new beginnings.

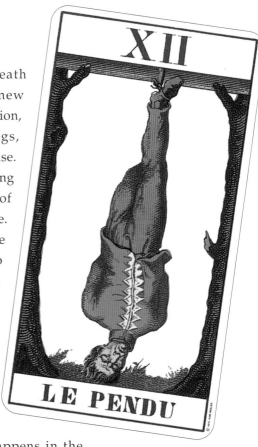

XIV *Temperance*

Moderation is called for and any excess avoided. The card indicates that the keynote is balance and harmony. Temperance is one of the virtues in the Tarot and as such is highly regarded. When it appears in a reading it brings a harmonious situation, friendship, compatibility and the positive results of a successful combination.

Temperance is an attitude to life which involves making best use of small things and cutting down waste as much as possible. Prudence and careful consideration bring success to a situation. Reflection makes it possible to see through false values. Patience must be observed as increase will develop in small ways and by small increments – 'Look after the pennies and the pounds will take care of themselves' is the message of this card.

Reversed Meaning

Extremes of behaviour are now suggested. There is the possibility of miserly behaviour, moderation in the extreme to the extent that any growth is stunted. Conversely, excess and waste may be indulged in. Situations and conflicts may be polarized.

XV *The Devil*

The Devil represents the human 'shadow', all the things that we regard as bad, which we don't see as existing in ourselves, only in other people. Slavery to the senses and baser instincts is the Devil's power, and this is his bondage. The pull of a temptation needs to be resisted, otherwise a dangerous situation will result. Licentious behaviour and imprisonment are also suggested. The Devil represents fate or 'karma', the inevitability of having to pay the price for past actions. When it appears in a reading, the debt is being called in.

Emotions of anger are aroused which can lead to violence if uncontrolled. In the end, the only person to be really hurt is the one who expresses anger and violence.

Reversed Meaning

Reversed, the influence of the Devil becomes superficial, indicating undignified behaviour and the influence of irresponsible pleasures. Pranks and impish behaviour lead to the appearance of foolishness. An overblown ego will now be taken down a peg or two.

XVI *The Tower or the House of God*

The lightning-struck tower brings destruction, disaster and at least setback, depending on other cards in the reading. The Tower represents rough justice, particularly in a situation where arrogance or pride have grown out of all proportion. Psychologically, inflation means having ideas above ones station, and the inflated bubble now bursts. An edifice is cast down. There is an implication that no matter how much you might try to protect yourself within a fortress, the sense of safety within is an illusion.

The appearance of the Tower can suggest a termination, perhaps of a friendship or relationship. Its influence is unexpected and in the extreme is a ruinous one. Its accompanying emotion is that of misery, and the eruption of this emotion can be enough to cause the ensuing destruction.

Reversed Meaning

Now the Tower represents the avoidance of a disaster, and a last-minute rescue is indicated. Indeed, rescue may not even be necessary for the impending disaster could be an illusion. The reversed meaning of the Tower is unique in that its interpretation takes on a most positive hue.

XVII *The Stars*

When the Stars appear, a bright future is indicated. They bring the blessings of the gods so that peace and tranquillity reign in the knowledge that all will be well. The rewards of past efforts and selfless behaviour come forth bringing a general feeling of happiness and wellbeing.

The person is now in a state of grace, which will only last for a while, but while it does, a sense of being in the right place at the right time prevails. A period of calm and stillness can be enjoyed, and the beauties of the world appreciated. Contemplating the stars themselves gives a feeling for the meaning of this card – the awareness of the infinite and its beauty, our tiny but important role in the great scheme of things.

Reversed Meaning

The atmosphere of peace and tranquillity is replaced in reversed position with a peace that is momentary, soon to be followed by feelings of sadness and a pensiveness about the future. There is a worry here that all is ultimately meaningless with an attendant loss of faith and sense of purpose.

XVIII *The Moon*

XIX *The Sun*

The Moon represents flux and change, the movement of a situation from one phase into the next. Adaptability to changing circumstances is required and the need to move with the times. The Moon indicates an ebb and flow so that it is necessary to go with the prevailing tide and not move against it. The Moon brings hidden mysteries, promptings from the unconscious, the pain and pleasure of childbearing.

The Moon brings unseen forces of transformation at work, natural forces which well up from out of the depths of the night. The Moon represents unconscious forces at work, the actions that we take, the feelings that we have, the thoughts we think, all of which pass through us as the Moon shines out from the blackness of night. The Moon brings with it a maternal instinct urging that caution in all matters is required.

Reversed Meaning

The Moon is in this position a devouring presence, eating up ones resources, ones energy. Loss of money is indicated, as too is illusion and deceit. A situation out of control, slipping through fingers is indicated. A warning of impending danger is given and that things are not as they seem to be on the surface. A time of decrease has now been entered. This is not necessarily 'bad', but should be understood as a phase to be passed through.

The Sun is a coordinating influence, ensuring that all factors in a situation work smoothly together. It shines with the light of reason and brings inspiration and a sense of 'life is for the living'. The appearance of the Sun brings with it will-power and a strong sense of purpose and is therefore a highly motivating influence. Accomplishment and success attend the Sun.

Its illuminating rays bring clarity to a situation and a sense of happiness. Whereas the Stars bring happiness and tranquillity, the Sun brings happiness and a period of fruitful activity, hard work with deserved rewards. Creativity is indicated and a flowering of manhood. As a symbol of male powers, the Sun suggests potency and strength.

Reversed Meaning

Now the Sun reversed is a portent of weakness, lack of coordination and sense of purpose. This is a failure languishing in wishful thinking and nostalgia for better times gone by.

XX *The Angel or Judgement*

As we approach the end of the cycle of Major Arcana cards, we come to the appearance of the card which represents a final decision, a final reward or punishment for previous deeds. The card can be seen as either good or bad, depending on its surrounding circumstances, and in the Tarot spread, the surrounding cards. Judgement indicates that a definite decision would be appropriate or that this is a time for determining end results. When more than one route has been available, there must be only one choice now.

Judgement is a portent of resurrection or rebirth, and the title of the Angel, suggests that perfection can be achieved, the perfect outcome, for good or ill.

Reversed Meaning

Indecision, delay and procrastination rule the situation, not poor judgement but no judgement at all. Far from perfect now, the situation is one where poor results are obtained, standards are low and end results are mediocre.

XXI *The World*

This is the final card in the Major Arcana and as such represents completion and the final triumph. This is the card of success when all ones ambitions are realized to the full. Everything falls into place forming a synthesis and wholeness. A situation is healed and resolves into a case of 'all's well that ends well'.

A time of great expansion is indicated and a situation that changes dramatically for the better. There is an opportunity to extend the boundaries of experience, to become worldly wise and, if circumstances are appropriate, to travel. The World may also bring a deeply religious sense and an awareness of the grand design of nature and the universe; a religious commitment may be in the air.

Reversed Meaning

Something is missing, an important factor which can throw life completely off balance. The result will be striving in vain, a sense of working hard and getting nowhere. There is a graceless attitude and a failure to accept limitations, which alienates one from other people, from the world at large. A mistaken sense of being denied ones rights prevails.

The Court Cards

King of Swords

The King of Swords represents a person who is at the peak of his mental powers. He is a ruler who will fight for his power particularly in debate. This person has achieved self-mastery, does not enjoy reflection and expresses dramatic decisive action. His weakness is a volatile temperament which means that his close relationships with other people can be full of turmoil and may be short lived.

He is a great 'parliamentarian' enjoying the heat of debate, but always having the last word on a matter. He is an upholder of law and order but is no traditionalist, always seeking to push back the boundaries of change. Making innovations as he goes, the King of Swords is versatile, forces the pace of change, and lacks the patience to see things through to the end before he is off on a new venture.

ROI DES ÉPÉES

Reversed Meaning

The King of Swords now represents tyranny and the abuse of power. He can be cruel in his attempts to gain mastery which will probably fail. He represents a mindless, pointless striving for control and fears its loss. The results of his actions will be the opposite of what he strives for, chaos and not order.

Queen of Swords

This is a woman capable of achieving the highest honours of success. In a man's world she can certainly hold her own and has great ability, a fine intelligence and a quick mind. She is powerful and her energy is ceaseless. Single-minded and with an awareness of the importance of attention to detail, the Queen of Swords is a persuasive person who possesses great powers of insight. It would be impossible to pull the wool over her eyes. Her skill is in manipulating opposing factions or forces to her own advantage, the type of person who can turn crisis and conflict into a situation that furthers her own plans.

Impressive in appearance, she is naturally the centre of attraction in any situation. It would be normal to feel nervous in her presence, as others may feel out of their depth with her.

Reversed Meaning

This is the destructive force of the female who believes that wrong has been done to her and should be revenged. The reversed Queen of Swords is a scheming woman who stoops to foul play and underhand measures to destroy the object of her hatred. She is being consumed by an inner passion, although outwardly you would not guess this for her actions are subtle, causing mayhem through the skillful employment of the half-truth.

Knight of Swords

The appearance of this card heralds an approaching battle, for the Knight of Swords is the archetypal warrior whose meaning in life is to fight. He knows no other way than to take up arms, confront the enemy head on and fight until he is victorious.

The Knight of Swords is not a mindless fighter, however, for he exhibits great intelligence and the ability to weigh up situations and see into the minds of the enemy. He will not fight a losing battle but will use his experience to weigh up carefully the risks, choose the best route to take, then fight to the death. He will rise to an occasion, expressing his best virtues in difficult situations. When his back is to the wall, then is the moment of his triumph.

To fight his battles successfully, the Knight of Swords needs a cause, something to fight for. In this he is not a leader but someone who upholds what he believes to be true and worthy.

Reversed Meaning

Reversed, the Knight of Swords indicates a person who is quick to fight battles which are unnecessary and which are ill thought through. His judgement of character is wanting and he is prejudiced and a bigot. He will not heed warnings and is likely to come unstuck through his own careless behaviour. He has little staying power and in a fight will give up when put under pressure.

Knave or Page of Swords

The Page of Swords is, like the Knight, a warrior, although he lacks initiative and experience. He needs to be told what to do, but then he will carry out instructions with understanding and diligence. He is an emissary who will negotiate well, exhibiting diplomacy and feeling for situations.

He is passionate in his beliefs, tending to see the world in black and white terms. He is a true friend who will do his best not to let you down. He has some knowledge of the world and feels easy in the company of those who have greater experience than he. He is youthful and far from being a seasoned campaigner, therefore holding ideals which may have to be modified in the light of future experience.

The Page of Swords expresses the qualities of a youth newly come to manhood holding knowledge which is based on learning and his passionate feelings. He has not yet tested his knowledge and feelings against the realities of life.

Reversed Meaning

The negative traits of the Page of Swords are a tendency to meddle in situations that are none of his business. He is prying, devious and vindictive, with an ability to seek out and play on the weaknesses of his adversaries. He also does not believe his own words.

ROI DE DENIER

REINE DE DENIER

King of Coins

This is not the leader of a cause but the leader of people – the pillar of society, a great worker for the community. He lacks intelligence and finesse but has a great command over the material affairs of the world, knows the way the system works and can work it well for his benefit. The King of Coins is at the peak of his powers as someone who can make things work. He has the ability to amass wealth and can turn any situation to a material advantage.

The King of Coins is generous and a philanthropist and will always support a good and worthy cause. His instincts are good and he makes a successful business-person with a purely pragmatic outlook on life, holding due reverence for the practical, no-nonsense approach.

The King of Coins is well fed and enjoys the fruits of his labours. There is nothing he likes better than to share a good meal and glass of wine with his next prospective business associate.

Reversed Meaning

The King of Coins is showing now the worst side of the materialist. He has no time at all for refinement, distrusting anything that speaks of the higher mind or artistic sensibilities. He is greedy, is easily bought and will exploit anyone or anything that comes his way. Prone to melancholy, he expresses inertia and is unable to adapt to change.

Queen of Coins

The Queen of Coins certainly enjoys her comforts. She enjoys wealth and abundance and is generous too, both materially and emotionally. She offers security and the enjoyment of life's physical pleasures. When she appears she brings with her bountiful delights. She is not overly intelligent nor artistic but has a feel for the good life. She also likes a grand occasion and will make grandiose gestures, although this does not mean she is wasteful. Her generosity is only given where she sees it to be deserved.

The Queen of Coins represents a person who is both rich and generous and offers great opportunities for growth. You are fortunate indeed to have such a person befriending you, for her generosity is limitless and comes from a nobility of purpose. She offers a fertile ground well worth tending for the fruits that it will bring forth. She offers security and support for those in her domain.

Reversed Meaning

The fertile ground is now barren and frozen. The Queen of Cups reversed has a cold heart and is miserly. There is distrust in the air, particularly for anything that she does not understand. She has the same preoccupation with wealth and the security it brings but now there is no enjoyment to be had from it.

Knight of Coins

This is a reliable person, hard-working and a supporter of the established order. He is dependable and patient. Given a job to do he will see it through to the end. He has high moral values and will defend them doggedly. The Knight of Coins does not act from his own initiative but will follow orders to the letter. He has a strong attachment to the daily realities of living but is by no means dour, taking life seriously, but having a happy disposition. He is content with his lot.

In a reading, the appearance of this card indicates someone who is dependable and can be relied upon to see a task through to its conclusion. It is a card which instills confidence. However, no-one can remain dependable all the time so watch out for the Knight of Coins' unpredictable streak.

Reversed Meaning

Here is someone who is a stickler for the rules. The Knight of Coins will play things by the book when it is entirely inappropriate to do so. He is just bloody-minded. Despite this rigid behaviour he is less than honest and lacks any real conviction in important matters, particularly those which involve close relationships.

Knave or Page of Coins

The Knave of Coins is a diligent and successful student with a thirst for knowledge, both academically and of the world at large. He sees himself, and indeed is, a reliable worker, always ready to absorb new information. He has a liking for the greater patterns in life and a feel for philosophy. There is a more introverted quality to this person than the other court cards in this suit, for he holds inside himself depths of thought and insight.

Although a willing worker, there is always much going on inside him which is hidden from view. He has a storehouse of knowledge but not yet the maturity to make best use of it. He is in the process of working things out inside himself.

CHEVALIER DES DENIERS

Reversed Meaning

The Knave of Coins now appears as a big fish in a small pond with ideas above his station which go beyond the reality of a situation. He enjoys wielding what little power he has. The reversed Knave of Coins is dull and thinks much more of his abilities than others do. He is pompous and ungenerous.

VALET DE DENIER

King of Staves or Batons

ROI DE BATON

This is the 'King Arthur' of the Tarot pack, a passionate warrior but peace loving and chivalrous. He has great qualities of leadership and inspires others to follow him. This inspiration comes from his ability to generate enthusiasm. He is quick witted, inventive and forceful.

The King of Batons has a strong intuitive faculty, is experienced in matters of life, both practical and emotional. He is cosmopolitan, feeling at home in any country and with any type of person. He has the ability to be successful at whatever he might turn his hand to, with the mind of an intellectual and the sensitivity and creative abilities of an artist.

When he appears in a reading, you can be sure that there is good advice to be taken from someone with valuable experience of the world. Look to him for invention and ways of dealing with a problem that needs lateral, creative thinking.

Reversed Meaning

The reversed King of Batons is a person who lacks vision and whose boundaries are limited. From being cosmopolitan, he now becomes parochial and narrow-minded. He is pompous and egocentric. There is prejudice expressed here and unreasonable intolerance.

Queen of Staves or Batons

The Queen of Batons is a symbol of fertility. She is the personification of female creativity. Her appearance in a spread brings with it initial success, and is therefore a good omen for new projects to get off the ground. She is by nature friendly and loving with a generous spirit.

She has an affinity for nature, feeling at home and at ease in the countryside, and has a remarkable encouraging effect on things that grow, whether plant, animal or human. She is worldly wise and knows that the act of giving brings rewards in terms of human friendship and devotion. A graceful patroness, the Queen of Batonss will bring success in business projects and will be formidable in opposition to anyone who crosses her path.

Reversed Meaning

If the Queen of Batons appears reversed, then her demeanour is one of offence taken over imagined wrongs. She is always expressing her hatred for all and sundry, proclaiming that wrongs have been done to her and that she will be avenged. As such, she is a dangerous influence, for the attacks that she makes will be unwarranted and therefore also unexpected. She has become an overbearing matriarch, unable to allow loved ones their emotional freedom.

REINE DE BÂTON

Knight of Staves or Batons

The Knight of Batons heralds a new opportunity, a chance for change, a situation that will now begin to move. He travels fast and has a fiery, intuitive mind. He lacks reason, but his intuitions are sound and can be relied upon. He has a quixotic temperament, one minute up, the next down and has an inability to remain still for long. As soon as he can, he will mount up and be off on the next quest for the Holy Grail.

He represents the traveller and heralds a journey or the arrival of someone who has been on a journey. He has a highly inventive mind but lacks practical knowledge. Therefore his forte is creating opportunity but not following it through with practicalities. When he appears, an opportunity should be grasped before it is too late, for in a flash he will be gone again. His presence can be unsettling for he urges change and the pulling up of ones roots.

Reversed Meaning

Now he sows the seeds of disharmony. He is mischievous liking to create conflict for the fun of it. He is wilfully destructive and will lead the unsuspecting astray. Reversed, he indicates the sowing of seeds of discontent, pushing for a change or move which is unnecessary.

Page of Staves or Batons

Here is the bringer of good news! A lively wit with boundless energy, he is a willing worker and guide. Trust him to show you the way or to lend a hand when your load gets too heavy. He is superb at sniffing out new ideas, new ways of doing things, endlessly making connections between people and places.

The Page of Batons is the Hermes of the Tarot pack, a gossip but by nature trustworthy and tireless in giving service to his masters. The Page of Batons has boundless enthusiasm and is the eternal optimist. His appearance symbolizes the genial stranger carrying important news. If it is life and energy that you wish to inject into a situation then he is the person to do it. Give him his head and he will turn up with all sorts of unexpected possibilities that come from afar.

CHEVALIER DES BÂTONS

Reversed Meaning

The news is now bad and the gossip malicious. The keynote of this card reversed is the destabilizing of a situation. Mistakenly believing himself to be profound, the Page of Batons is superficial, speaks with a forked tongue, propagates misleading information.

VALET DE BÂTON

King of Cups

Skilled in the ways of the world, the King of Cups is a brilliant negotiator with the ability to control and manoeuvre situations, emotions, to suit his own requirements and to increase his power. He is, however, not extroverted, so that he remains a private person, his inner thoughts and motivations being held close to his chest.

He instinctively works in secret and this can inspire mistrust. He is a respected figure but this is the result of a charismatic aura and not because he is loved. He arrives in a position of authority not by his own achievements but through the efforts of others. He has the ability to channel the abilities and talents of others into his own direction, using others to build his power base. In his presence you will always feel that he knows what is going on inside you but that his inner world remains a closed door.

Reversed Meaning

Any moral sense is now lost so that the King of Cups manipulates others purely for self-aggrandizement and when he has taken what he needs, then he casts off those he has used without a thought. The reversal of this card indicates moral bankruptcy. There is a danger of being caught up by him in a web of cunning and deceit which leads to a downfall.

Queen of Cups

The Queen of Cups has a great artistic gift. She is the poet, musician, artist, actress, with a natural talent to go with her natural beauty. The embodiment of female intuition she is adaptable, malleable, able to bend with the wind, to be all things to all people. The presence of this card in a reading indicates the involvement of a person endowed with the art of graceful living. She can be a siren, if not a loving partner.

The Queen of Cups brings out the poet and romantic in you, loving to be wooed with the pleasures of culture and beauty. She has a mystical aura and is known to be prophetic, her prophecies stemming from her natural attunement to the emotional nature. In her presence, expect to be entranced by beauty, to swear your allegiance and devotion. This is the indicator of someone falling in love with an ideal.

Reversed Meaning

The call of the siren now leads to destruction. Her voice is still alluring but the temptations she offers are idle fantasies. Her words cannot be trusted. Reversed, the Queen of Cups can change her mind, change her opinions, change her loyalties at the drop of a hat. She acts as if she has talent but in fact has none. There is a tendency now to emotional excesses and temper tantrums.

Knight of Cups

The Knight of Cups brings a proposal, an invitation or an opportunity. His words are seductive and his judgement is clouded by emotion. It is therefore right to approach him with some caution. A situation may demand careful and rational thought, in which case his appeals should be considered with great care. It is all too easy to be carried along by his enthusiasm.

This character is a romantic, with high ideals, easily led and an opportunist, in need of constant stimulation. His appearance portends a favourable event but take care not to be swept up by it without a thought for practicalities. These are unimportant to the Knight of Cups who only sees the romantic side of things and does not take the practical consequences into account. He is a little too quick to celebrate his successes, looking only on the positive side and conveniently ignoring the rest.

Reversed Meaning

He has, in the reversed position, an inability to discern where the truth ends and fantasy begins, holding out false promises. He represents a situation which looks good but, behind the facade, all is far from well. He also has a tendency to over-sentimentality and shallowness. He is a character not to be trusted.

Page of Cups

The Page of Cups brings the birth of new feelings, representing youthful enthusiasm. He is introverted, quiet, given to periods of quiet contemplation and solitary study. He is painstaking and is a fund of useful knowledge which he will release freely when asked.

The Page of Cups is without guile, is innocent of any of the world's evils. He is capable of deep affection and is easily hurt if slighted or rejected. He is the youth who has just discovered the joys of poetry and immerses himself in its pleasures. When he appears in a reading it suggests casting off life's worries and cares to enable deep feelings to well to the surface, bringing with them a new sense of creativity and wonder. The Page of Cups appears when it is right to trust feelings and to give them full play.

CHEVALIER DES COUPES

Reversed Meaning

Superficiality is the essence of this card now, for the Page of Cups now lacks depth and experience, and the ability to apply himself to anything. He is too easily distracted. His attraction, as a beautiful, romantic youth is seductive, but once drawn to him you will find there is nothing in his empty head.

VALET DE COUPE

The Minor Arcana

Ace of Swords

Keynote – Triumph
Number Symbolism – Birth

This is the sword of righteousness bringing victory, success and triumph. The overall tenor of the reading will indicate whether this is for good or ill. This is an indicator that enterprises will succeed despite the odds against. It brings an irresistible force which will result in the removal of constraints and the breaking through into a new phase of operations.

Success is achieved through the force of will power and there is an element of the zealot in this process. The Ace of Swords brings the overthrow of the old order and the establishment of the new. It is the antithesis of the *status quo* and its action is such that once under way, nothing can stop this irresistible force for change. The Sword brings a breakdown in the order of things so that a new order can take hold.

Reversed Meaning

This symbol of wanton destruction and the abuse of power leads to unjust actions, and change for the sake of change. There is violence and the use of brute force. It indicates that the current course of action is leading to self-destruction.

Two of Swords

Keynote – Friendship
Number Symbolism – Polarity

There is a balanced relationship between polar opposites indicated here, perhaps the relationship between teacher and pupil, or between elder and youngster. The forging of such a relationship results in a particular form of fruitful friendship where both parties benefit, the one by gaining knowledge from the more experienced partner, the other by passing on wisdom to another generation.

The card indicates also that such a relationship may be frowned upon by the outside world, so that decisions have to be made in the face of adversity. The card asks for equilibrium between opposing forces in life so that progress can be made. This card is a counterfoil to the Ace of Swords, creating balance between opposing forces, while the Ace comes down firmly in favour of one side creating change.

Reversed Meaning

The card now indicates disharmony between the polar opposites. There may be a false friendship, or a relationship that founders through mistrust or disloyalty. Disruption and discord result from the deliberate stirring up of trouble.

Three of Swords

Keynote – Strife
Number Symbolism – Resolution

All is upheaval, discord and strife when this card appears. It is not so negative as it seems though, for the strife is necessary to produce something better in the end. The number symbolism indicates that two forces are in conflict, while a third holds them in check. This suggests that the resolution of a conflict should be sought in a third factor, not in the opposing forces themselves. The card suggests that an outside influence needs to come into the equation before the strife will cease. The triangle thus established will be in balance but contain great activity, a potentially dangerous situation.

Quarrels and separations will ensue before the new and better order is established.

Reversed Meaning

In its reversed position, the triangle is in a much more stable condition, so that within a time of struggle and strife a period of peaceful respite can be found. Another possibility exists here in that all partnerships and relationships within the triangle can be dissolved, bringing the situation to a sorry conclusion.

Four of Swords

Keynote – Respite
Number Symbolism – Healing

All of the swords cards tell of strife, whether creative or destructive but in this card is respite from the struggle. The Four of Swords indicates a necessary period of calm and withdrawal from the battle. It suggests the opportunity for rest and recuperation before the fray is entered once more. It may indicate also an illness which enforces a period of rest and healing.

The peace is not a natural one, however, and is held together by rule of law and order. Without this show of force, the peace will collapse. In a mundane sense, the card suggests that one should take a holiday, but that there will be pressure against this. A time of self-imposed retreat is necessary.

Reversed Meaning

When the card is reversed, the retreat is not self-imposed but is forced. There is a reluctance to face up to problems and a failure of nerve is indicated. Enforced seclusion or confinement bring about the heaviness of depression and loss of the will to continue.

Five of Swords

Keynote – Futility

Number Symbolism – Creativity

At first glance, the keynote and number symbolism for this card seem to be contradictory, but this is not the case. When this card appears it suggests that actions are futile and that accepting the inevitable and giving up a useless course of action is necessary. The reason for this is important. The card suggests that a dead end has been entered and that another route should be taken, thus releasing the creative process once more. Defeat or loss must be accepted and another route tried.

Refusal to accept a situation will lead to failure and dishonour, but acceptance and a new direction will bring future success. Limitations must be accepted and pride swallowed.

Reversed Meaning

Failure is the result of indecision and weakness. There may be treachery afoot and malice, particularly in someone involved closely with your affairs. This is a card warning of the actions of others that can lead to disastrous effects.

Six of Swords

Keynote – A battle won

Number Symbolism – Insight

Immediate problems are solved, a battle won, but this is not the end of the war, so strife will continue. Through a daring and adventurous act comes success and this is a breakthrough, hence the number symbolism of 'insight'. The breakthrough leads to new realizations and progress can be made as a result. The card may indicate that movement away from the field of conflict is now possible but that the conflict itself does not disappear. Movement may mean a change in circumstances, greener fields, or it could also mean a physical move, a change of location.

The Six of Swords indicates the escape from a tense and stressful situation or relationship in favour of one which is more harmonious. The ability to move in this favourable direction is brought about by a decisive and brave act.

Reversed Meaning

No sooner is a problem solved than another appears in its place. It is necessary to keep up the struggle otherwise all will be lost. There is no progress now, despite much effort, rather like treading water. If effort ceases then drowning ensues.

Seven of Swords

Keynote – Foresight
Number Symbolism – Contemplation, inner work

This card advises that success is achievable in the face of opposition and conflict. The way to achieve this success is not through head-on confrontation but by stealth and circuitous routes. Careful deliberation and a rational response are called for, even cunning.

The odds are overwhelming with obvious defeat if the enemy is fought on their terms. However, success is possible if prudence is exercised. The way to move forward can be found through meditation, through examining ones inner motives and drives and allowing creative solutions to arise from the unconscious. Alert awareness will make the route to be taken clear.

Reversed Meaning

The reversed card indicates that there is a failure to carry through to its conclusion the correct course of action, perhaps through accepting ill-informed advice or a failure of nerve or effort when bravery is called for.

Eight of Swords

Keynote – End of adversity
Number Symbolism – Totality

Major difficulties occur, particularly those that result from not being dealt with earlier. Problems pile up and fate seems to be against you. Although the interpretation of this card suggests that all is trouble and strife, there is a definite hint that the end of a cycle is approaching, that the final push is on. The cycle has not yet ended so all responsibilities that have not been faced up to come crowding in.

Changes for the better are underlying the adverse surface circumstances but they will not automatically come to the surface. It is necessary to complete the cycle properly, to tackle unfinished business no matter how onerous. There is an indication in this card that out of emotional difficulties and even great loss, comes the strength to face the world anew.

Reversed Meaning

The effect is of ceaseless and unrewarded effort. A lot of energy is spent in going nowhere, but if the effort ceases, then you sink. Stopping in your efforts now will bring disaster. Even if you seem to be getting nowhere, it is wise to continue. Frustrated actions can lead to depression.

Nine of Swords

Keynote – Martyrdom
Number Symbolism – Completion

You name it, this card has it – deception, disappointment, failure, cruelty, violence, but fear not, there is a way of dealing with it. Suffering is the order of the day. This is the card of crucifixion, the card of the martyr. Out of this suffering will come new life, but for the moment, the way to combat life's evils is by silent acceptance and purposeful inaction. Obedience is called for, any action which opposes the *status quo* being quashed mercilessly.

Mental anguish can result from the cruel blows of fate and there may be over-reaction to a difficulty with violent outbursts of frustrated rage. In this state of helpless martyrdom, others will seem to have the success that you feel you deserve, leading to jealousy and hatred.

Reversed Meaning

In reversed position, the difficulties suggested by the upright position are accompanied by complete isolation from the possibility of help or assistance. Comfort is unobtainable.

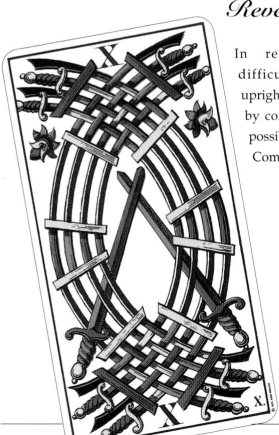

Ten of Swords

Keynote – Ruin
Number Symbolism – Conclusion

As a suit, the swords indicate strife and opposition and with the final card comes the final outcome. The bottom has now been reached, things cannot get any worse so the only way now is up and out. The degree of this 'bottoming out' depends on the circumstances being considered and the other cards in a reading. The meaning of the card can range from total loss and disaster to a minor cause for concern. The point is that the Ten of Swords represents a turning point at the bottom of a cycle of progress.

Traditionally, its appearance suggests that a group of people are subject to this process rather than an individual. An interesting point to note is that the final calamity is brought about through choice, not by the conspiracy of events.

Reversed Meaning

Unfortunately, any success which is gained is illusory and is not a success at all. The facing of reality ensues, the reality being that strife and conflict continue. Any gain will soon be lost.

Ace of Coins

Keynote – Prosperity
Number Symbolism – Birth

Material wealth and comfort are the rewards given by this card. The good life ensues and gain is assured. This card suggests great success in material matters and that investments will be favourably rewarded. There is a great strength associated with the Ace of Coins in that its interpretation is the ability to remain steadfast and rooted in the face of any opposition. Standing firm in the face of adversity brings success and gain.

Material gain and security will not be fleeting as this card marks the beginning of a cycle, thus getting things off to a good start. It is possible that money is not indicated here for wealth can be interpreted as a feeling as much as a measurement of quantity. Spiritual as well as material wealth may be indicated. Basically, whatever makes you feel well off!

Reversed Meaning

Lack of imagination and materialism are indicated, together with an inability to give credence to anything that does not impinge on the physical senses. Greed, waste and disrespect for the earth's resources are common, as too are extremes of stubborn behaviour.

Two of Coins

Keynote – Movement
Number Symbolism – Polarity

When this card appears, movement and change lie ahead, all part of a natural process. When something has reached an extreme, a conclusion, or one end of a polarity, movement does not cease but flows back in the opposite direction as sure as night follows day. Plan for change to ensure that success continues. The indications are that one should not remain in the same place, nor resist the winds of change, but go with them.

There is an interesting aspect to this card for it not only heralds natural change but also the birth of new and unforeseen circumstances. This too is in accord with the philosophy of change from one polar opposite to the other, for although this might seem to be a predictable process, predictability has its polar opposite too! It is best to plan for fluctuating fortunes and to be ready for the unforeseen.

Reversed Meaning

Reckless action leads to loss. Warnings of impending difficulty are ignored at ones peril. Opportunities for future success are missed. There is a tendency to be in the wrong place at the wrong time.

Three of Coins

Keynote – Establishment
Number Symbolism – Resolution

Hard work is well worth while when this card appears, for it is rewarded with success, achievement and progress. Skill exercised is appreciated by others who will support any venture undertaken. This is a time for beginning and establishing new projects, provided that the skills to make them work are available. It is the card of the successful business person or crafts person who will receive just rewards for his or her endeavours.

The card suggests the early and successful phase of a project or enterprise which will flourish in the future, so that any business venture undertaken is sure to expand with time. The card indicates that all the factors involved are properly balanced creating a harmonious work environment. The emphasis is on skill and hard work, laying foundations for later refinement.

Reversed Meaning

The reversed Three of Coins indicates that effort is being put into a project that will not be successful. Others can see this and offer advice which fails to move an obstinate persistency. Just criticism follows.

Four of Coins

Keynote – Stability
Number Symbolism – Healing

The Four of Coins brings a period of success and wealth. Projects flourish and become well established. Any obstacles to success in the material sphere will be removed and transactions completed through reasonable negotiation. There is power in the background, the power which comes with material wealth and security. The judicious exercising of this power is helpful in bringing positive results.

There may be a tendency to unnecessary amassing of wealth and an attitude of greed with its associated miserly behaviour. This will be so if other cards in the reading tend to support it.

Reversed Meaning

Fear of losing what has been gained, results in an overprotective attitude and the inability to 'let go' or delegate to others. Change is necessary and this fear of loss prevents necessary changes from taking place. A decentralization of power is asked for which is not forthcoming.

Five of Coins

Keynote – Material worries
Number Symbolism – Creativity

This card is usually most unwelcome for it heralds a period of great activity which results in material loss, unemployment and much worry about money. Despite the negative interpretation of this card there is an up side. New relationships will be formed with others in the same situation and these will lead to new possibilities in different directions than before. The opening up of new avenues will accompany any loss.

The card does not indicate helpless inactivity but that circumstances are being broken down, put in a chaotic melting pot with the promise that new life will eventually emerge from it. This is a creative process, loss in this case being a herald of gain.

Reversed Meaning

It is imperative not to continue with the current course of action as it is doomed to failure. Failure can be avoided but there is a tendency to obstinacy in the face of the inevitable. There is a failure to see what is really going on.

Six of Coins

Keynote – Generosity
Number Symbolism – Insight

The Six of Coins demonstrates philanthropy and generosity. This comes as the result of material gain and security in material matters. There is a desire to share with others less fortunate and to support worthy projects. It may indicate that loans are repaid or that loans applied for are successfully obtained.

The time has come now to shift the emphasis from building oneself up to assisting others. Gratitude should be shown for past favours. Kindness and charity are appropriate particularly if hard-heartedness has been shown in the past. The card indicates that it is appropriate to become a patron or to accept patronage, depending on ones personal circumstances. Money matters are stable enough to support this without being knocked off balance.

Reversed Meaning

There is a refusal to help others, a loan declined, a project in need of support refused. Carelessness with money is likely, resulting in loss. Theft is indicated.

Seven of Coins

Keynote – Taking care
Number Symbolism – Contemplation, inner work

This card appears at a fairly late stage in a project or undertaking involving material affairs. It indicates that there are difficulties occurring that are not insurmountable. However, diligence and care should be taken. It is necessary to continue working hard at achieving ones goals. It is a warning that the future is bringing new difficulties, loss and danger but that application and diligence can avert these problems.

The Seven of Coins means that all the effort put into a project in the past will be wasted if effort ceases. There is a tendency to inertia which must be combated. The honeymoon period has passed so that the world does not look so tempting any more. You would rather be doing something else but must stick to your guns if future calamity is to be avoided.

Reversed Meaning

There is an inability to exercise patient care and to continue diligent application. The result is loss and failure. The will has gone to succeed so that stagnation follows.

Eight of Coins

Keynote – Reward
Number Symbolism – Totality

A change in circumstances brings material reward, particularly through hard work and application. This is the card which indicates that the expenditure of physical energy is well worth while in bringing a favourable change and ensuring that success will be long lasting. Any skill should be turned towards profitable ends although skill is not necessarily called for.

The point of the Eight of Coins is that hard labour brings reward so it represents a time for keeping ones nose to the grind stone. Where money is concerned there are no illusions about the gaining of wealth. It all comes down to hard work now.

Reversed Meaning

Mistaken short-term policies lead to long-term failure. Reversed, the Eight of Coins indicates shortsightedness and a grasping at immediate gain without accounting for the long-term effects of this. There is an indication that resources are diverted improperly or are misappropriated, meaning that illegal or immoral financial dealings are afoot.

Nine of Coins

Keynote – Dormancy
Number Symbolism – Completion

An analogy will best describe the meaning of the Nine of Coins. A time of dormancy, a fallow period is required. Rather like cooking a good casserole, once the ingredients have been mixed and cooked, a further period of cooking is required to allow the flavours to blend. All that is required is that the pot is left for a while to simmer slowly on its own. The card indicates that in the material sphere this is exactly what is required.

There is a period of material security and comfort. Sound administrative ability shows that the right course of action is rest and respite. Allowing others to do the hard work is appropriate while you enjoy the fruits of your labours. No further gain can be achieved.

Reversed Meaning

The stability of the present situation will not last because it has been achieved through devious means. Self-satisfaction is inappropriate for there are those who will create stormy and destructive circumstances. They feel aggrieved because any gain has been based on their misfortunes. Idleness will be rewarded with loss.

Ten of Coins

Keynote – Family security
Number Symbolism – Conclusion

This is the card of family wealth and indicates that money or property is passing from one generation to another. Inheritance is a possibility, as too is a redistribution of wealth. The Ten of Coins represents family prosperity and good fortune based on the establishing of a tradition.

Blood ties are all-important in material affairs and one should not look beyond these for support or gain. The effects of successive generations are felt. Current circumstances are surrounded by family affections. The card can indicate that it is appropriate to pass on responsibility and power to those younger, or to receive it from ones elders, depending on circumstances.

Reversed Meaning

This reversal brings the ending of a long-standing tradition and heralds difficulties associated with heirs and lines of succession. The reversed Ten of Coins indicates the loss of family wealth or status. Gambling with family resources brings about their loss.

Ace of Cups

Keynote – Love

Number Symbolism – Birth

This is the prime significator of love and fulfilment. It is a cornucopia overflowing with the gifts of emotional and spiritual life. The Ace of Cups brings a feeling that the world is a wonderful place to live in and that life couldn't be better.

The consummation of a partnership is indicated, marriage and the creation of a family. This card accompanies the beginning of a whole new phase in life and indicates a period of great fruitfulness. If appropriate, predictions can be made of marriage and the bearing of children. A great emphasis should be placed on nurturing feelings of faithfulness and the promise of an enduring partnership, which will bring nourishment and protection to the parties involved. The Ace of Cups is the Holy Grail of the Tarot cards! It is worth questing for and when it appears provides endless nourishment for the soul.

Reversed Meaning

In its reversed position, the contents of the cup empty themselves out and are wasted. The card now indicates barrenness and the failure of a relationship. The accompanying feeling is of despair and a loss of faith. It can also mean unrequited love, or passion that trickles away through lack of awareness or attention.

Two of Cups

Keynote – Partnership

Number Symbolism – Polarity

The Two of Cups indicates the creation of a new partnership after a period of conflict. The resolution of this conflict brings a mutual balancing of previously separate, polarized entities. The result can be the signing of a treaty or even marriage.

The ending of rivalry or feuding takes place and is transformed into an agreement of mutually beneficial proportions. If interpreted on a romantic level, The Two of Cups means love at first sight, the recognition of a soul-mate that was not seen before and the forming of a sexual/emotional trust. The card suggests the tying of bonds by mutual happy agreement, for the parties involved now have an emotional affinity and understanding of one another. Mutual trust exists where before there was disharmony and distrust. The bonds that are formed are invisible but strong and not to be broken.

Reversed Meaning

Unfaithfulness in a personal relationship is indicated. At worst there may be divorce which comes as the result of the betrayal of trust, jealousy and irresponsible behaviour. Something which is valuable is thrown away.

Three of Cups

Keynote – Fruition
Number Symbolism – Resolution

A happy event can be celebrated when this card appears for it signifies family matters and the realization of hopes and wishes. This means the arrival of a child of love, born from the fruits of earlier labours. This card rules the maternal instinct, bringing it to the forefront. The accompanying feelings are of love, trust, stability and harmony. It is a card which brings the healing of ills. Family matters are to the fore and, despite the happy event, a period of hard work and commitment lies ahead.

Although the suit of Cups deals with emotional matters, this card indicates that practical affairs must be considered so that the future situation remains secure. The Three of Cups comes bearing gifts which will mean future responsibilities and hard work. This should not detract from the current happy situation.

Reversed Meaning

The pleasures of life are indulged in excessively. These pleasures are self-indulgent and superficial. There is nothing to be gained from them other than immediate gratification. There is no love involved, although the emotions expressed may be excessive.

Four of Cups

Keynote – Familiarity
Number Symbolism – Healing

The Four of Cups represents the pinnacle of an emotional relationship. No further progress is being made and hence the seeds of future discontent can be sown. Although all seems well on the surface, there is a growing dissatisfaction which may not be at all obvious. Doubt about the future brings a sense of uneasiness and the lack of progress creates feelings of stagnation and boredom.

This is a card which brings an opportunity, for it points to the fact that although emotional needs have been met, the future may bring a change caused by an underlying feeling of going nowhere. The opportunity lies in the awareness of this situation – steps can be taken to avoid future disruption and to inject new life into a situation. Steps must be taken to rejuvenate an affair of the heart, for example, for passivity will allow the situation to develop into deterioration. It is a case of familiarity breeds contempt.

Reversed Meaning

Reversed, the Four of Cups indicates that something enters a stagnating situation, shakes it up and turns it upside down! The result is rejuvenation of a flagging relationship as new possibilities push it through into a new phase. If other cards support a more negative interpretation, complacent over-indulgence leads to jaded ill-health.

Five of Cups

Keynote – Reassessment

Number Symbolism – Creativity

The emotional cups are overturned presenting a situation in a state of flux and change where some form of loss is inevitable. In a relationship, this can be disturbing and bring feelings of fear and resentment. All is not lost, however, for the situation is a changing one and brings the opportunity to reassess current circumstances and make appropriate changes for the better. Without a good, long, hard look at what needs to be done, the situation will deteriorate.

The message of this card is that, if no action is taken, then there will be disharmony, so it is well worth putting some effort into reorganizing, rearranging, restructuring, so that the future will take on a more positive hue. This will be a worrying time, for gain in the future cannot be achieved without loss in the present. Feelings of sadness and disappointment will ensue.

Reversed Meaning

There is an inability to face up to difficult facts and accept the harsh realities of a situation. There will be nostalgia for a situation now gone by and a tendency to live in the past. Hopes that things will turn out well are wishful thinking.

Six of Cups

Keynote – Memories

Number Symbolism – Insight

An interpretation of this card should place an emphasis on matters of the past which are influencing current events. There is an opportunity to savour present pleasures which are the result of past situations. The card represents happiness built on past efforts and the realization of a dream. There are also new opportunities in the air for future growth – past, present and future are all represented here at a blending point.

Feelings of harmony and well-being pervade the atmosphere, although there may well be nostalgia too for times gone by. This is a time for recognizing the important influences of the past, even of childhood and the early home life. Realizations of why things are the way they are will arise with the understanding of these early influences. The result of this understanding will be a renewed activity in the present as rejuvenating opportunities lead the way into the future.

Reversed Meaning

The Six of Cups now indicates an inability to adapt to changing circumstances and that there is a nostalgia which is strong enough to make one live in the past, an unrealistic state of affairs.

Seven of Cups

Keynote – Choice
Number Symbolism – Contemplation, inner work

With the appearance of the Seven of Cups comes the need to make a choice from several possibilities. The making of the correct choice will lead to great success, but it is not an obvious one to make. The card is surrounded by an aura of illusion, falsehood and mystery. It will be all too easy to make the wrong decision so careful consideration is called for. What is needed is a time of inner reflection and total honesty with oneself. Examining ones inner motives and drives through quiet contemplation will be the way to determine the correct choice to be made.

A great deal of perception is required and the ability to see through illusions and falsehoods. Beware the imagination playing tricks, making it difficult to sort out the real from the unreal, the true from the false. Such inner perception can bring the rewards of a mystical experience as a penetration is made into the nature of reality.

Reversed Meaning

The reversed position now indicates pure fantasy and false hopes, particularly where feelings and matters of the heart are concerned. For the few it can also mean great determination and resolve to overcome illusion.

Eight of Cups

Keynote – Capitulation
Number Symbolism – Totality

Strong feelings which have not been heeded or which have not been acted on now force their way to the surface and the enquirer gives in to them. The result is change, the severing of a relationship with the past and a turning away from established patterns to create something new. There will be the abandonment of a person or situation from which the enquirer simply walks away.

Others may see this as a foolhardy act based entirely on self-delusion. The fact is that even if this be true, the act is necessary in order to achieve future progress. It is a case of the end justifying the means. The experience is of giving in to external forces and internal feelings, allowing them to hold sway. The resulting changes will be in the sphere of affections and personal relationships where emotional bonds exist.

Reversed Meaning

The reversed Eight of Cups suggests the abandonment of an established love in favour of one which is an impossible ideal. Dissatisfaction underlies this action. This is the leopard trying in vain to change its spots!

Nine of Cups

Keynote – Goodwill

Number Symbolism – Completion

This is one of the most harmonious of the Tarot cards to arise in a reading, for feelings of inner contentment, fulfilment and enjoyment spill out to create an atmosphere of goodwill and sharing. An overall sense of well-being is infectious and permeates the surrounding situation – people respond positively to it. This is a time for pleasurable pursuits, bringing feelings of emotional wealth and spiritual well-being. The feeling that arises is of being at the right place at the right time.

Any outstanding difficulties or arguments are resolved at this time. Forgiveness and reconciliation are in the air leading to the beginning of a new phase of development. Where trust in a person or relationship is required, then it will not be misplaced.

Reversed Meaning

Self-satisfaction and over-confidence lead to mis-judgements about the motives of others. The result is that ones hospitality, generosity and openness are abused. Over-confidence then turns into emotional insecurity.

Ten of Cups

Keynote – Love

Number Symbolism – Conclusion

Feelings of love are genuinely expressed to another and are reciprocated. The Ten of Cups signifies harmony and happiness in a mutual relationship. There is a true blending of opposites to form a whole, a complete unit. Family life blossoms bringing feelings of joy and happiness. A perfect balance is struck.

Befriending ones inner self results in the creation of a beautiful friendship with another. There is a depth of spiritual meaning in this card such that love may be expressed not only for another creature of flesh and blood, but one with soul and spirit too. This creates a sense of religious feeling, even the falling in love with a religious ideal. The Ten of Cups brings the opportunity to experience a peaceful and secure environment. 'Starting a new life together' is a phrase which sums up this card.

Reversed Meaning

Disruption and emotional turbulence arise so that nothing runs smoothly. Offers of love and emotional support are rejected. Disharmony and quarrels bring trouble and strife.

Ace of Batons

Keynote – New Beginnings
Number Symbolism – Birth

The keynote and number symbolism for this card coincide exactly. This is the card of 'the worm turning'. When it appears in a spread something is being born. This should be interpreted on the appropriate level – it could be a physical child or the birth of a new idea. The Batons represent the fires of creativity and inspiration and the Ace means that this experience is felt with great force.

On an inner level, the Ace of Batons brings the faculty of intuition and imagination into play, for it is through these that anything new first comes into being. New beginnings, new projects, a fresh start, all these are indicated. Inspiration and enthusiasm are the order of the day and the foundation of something that promises future success and abundance. Look for inventiveness and innovation of some sort which come from giving free play to the imagination.

Reversed Meaning

A false start is indicated when the Ace of Batons is in reversed position. This may come from over-confidence and complacency resulting in initial failure. Lack of inspiration and an arid mind are also indicated.

Two of Batons

Keynote – Strength
Number Symbolism – Polarity

Great strength is shown by this card, the wielding of which brings success. Courage and boldness are indicated leading to the establishment of strong leadership. Just authority and the wielding of power which benefits all is indicated. High ideals and motives are behind the strength indicated by this card so that the results are seen to be good. Success comes through the application of courage and boldness and the ability to ward off opposition. The card also indicates that wisdom has been earned through experience and this can now be appreciated by others.

Responsibility is called for because the enquirer is now in a position of power and authority. The mantle of responsibility is accepted and worn with great dignity. The indication is of the initial stages of an accomplishment, the acceptance of a new role with the power to affect the lives of others. The ability to overcome obstacles is strong. There is restlessness associated with this card, perhaps a keen desire to get on with things.

Reversed Meaning

Although strength and boldness are still here together with the desire to make progress, actions are blocked and delayed. The result can be the application of force which only brings disillusionment and a loss of faith.

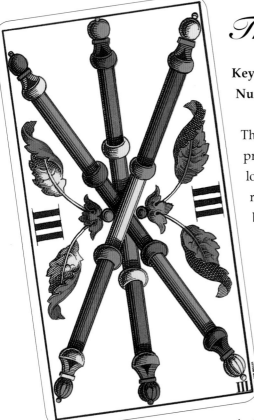

Three of Batons

Keynote – Dreams into Reality
Number Symbolism – Resolution

The winning or achievement of a great prize accompanies this card. After a long struggle the dream is turned into a reality – a difficult thing to accomplish, but now all the difficulties are over and the prize won.

Conviction, enterprise and effort are rewarded by witnessing the original inspiration now being turned into a reality and put into practice. The only rider that is attached to this card is that there is much more that can be achieved. Now is the time to bask in feelings of glory and self satisfaction, but this will pass and the need for further hard work and commitment will come.

The achievement is not the pinnacle of the mountain which is being climbed but does reveal that the ultimate prize is now possible. Enjoy the feeling of personal satisfaction in success and then move on.

Reversed Meaning

A factor enters the situation which will knock you off your balance. The reversed position suggests a lack of ability to make a link between the imagination and the real world. The result is frustration and a retreat into a fantasy land. Great schemes come to nothing. Assistance from others should be considered very carefully as there may be ulterior motives involved.

Four of Batons

Keynote – Satisfaction
Number Symbolism – Healing

This is the card which belongs to the successful person, particularly in affairs of career. It indicates professionalism and the ability to turn ideas into reality. There is an ability to work well with other people and the atmosphere surrounding this card is harmonious, productive and prosperous for all parties involved.

The Four of Batons is a card of civilized behaviour, of the cosmopolitan who is at home in varied company and can express mental agility. There is a feeling for the good things in life, for art, culture and refinement. Often accompanying this card is a romantic relationship where both parties are in tune with one another because of mutual interests, particularly in the field of culture and the arts. Pleasurable, amorous adventures are undertaken while feeling at peace with the world and with oneself. Accompanying this is achievement in the realm of ideas, with two minds inspired and thinking alike.

Reversed Meaning

Snobbery and the ivory tower are associated with the reversed Four of Batons. Unnecessary airs and graces mean that there is a cutting off from the realities of everyday life and the creation of an 'us and them' situation. Feelings of superiority are completely inappropriate the result being that support is withdrawn and desires remain unfulfilled.

Five of Batons

Keynote – Obstacles
Number Symbolism – Creativity

Here you have a fight on your hands – not in a physical sense, but mental agility and decisive action are required to overcome obstacles. It is no use trying to avoid conflicts which must be surmounted before any future progress can be made. The flow of a project will be cut short, through circumstances which were not foreseen, and it is now necessary to regroup and reconsider the course of action from here on.

There is a feeling of being at odds with the world, when, for no apparent reason, circumstances change from running smoothly to seeming that everything is causing problems. This is probably not the case but only seems so because of a particular stumbling block. Ingenuity is called for to solve the problem, so new avenues of thought and new possibilities should be explored. The correct attitude is to go with the number symbolism and regard the situation as an impulse for creative thought, so that once conflicts have been quelled, progress will continue with new vigour.

Reversed Meaning

When the card is upright, conflict may be temporary if dealt with firmly – but reversed, the conflicts and difficulties are set to continue for some time to come. Things go from bad to worse and a relationship enters a downward spiral. No support from others is forthcoming.

Six of Batons

Keynote – Victory
Number Symbolism – Insight

The message of this card is quite definite. After a long period of struggle, a great victory has been won. This has been achieved not by force but by skillful negotiation, by using brain power. Both hard work and originality have been employed to secure this victory such that all those who were in opposition either accept defeat or come to support the cause.

There is a sense of satisfaction at a job well done, an inner knowing that all the actions of the past have now been vindicated. It was not possible to foresee the outcome, but now it has come, it all seems clear and inevitable. Congratulations will be forthcoming from colleagues and adversaries alike. The card heralds the arrival of excellent news and deserved acclamation. This success has been hard won and it is possible now to bask in a little glory, so make the most of it.

Reversed Meaning

In its reversed position, the Six of Batons represents fears about the outcome of a situation, fears of defeat and, significantly, fears of success too. This card can suggest a situation where a successful outcome is possible but the enquirer is their own worst enemy.

Seven of Batons

Keynote – Determination
Number Symbolism –
Contemplation, inner work

While the Six of Batons represents victory, the Seven suggests the possibility of victory. The present situation requires great courage and determination – inner strength – if the end result is to be positive. There is much competition and adversity surrounding the nature of this card. To deal with this, fortitude and sustained effort are required. Despite great obstacles there is the promise of success just around the corner.

Even the difficulties of life which seem to be more to do with fate and sheer bad luck are now surmountable through personal effort and diligence. Nothing is too difficult a problem that a way cannot be found to deal with it. The inner strength to do so comes from quiet contemplation and the ability to look long and hard at a situation before acting with strength of will. The situation lends one a sense of authority, the ability to communicate and to teach others what is required.

Reversed Meaning

The reversed Seven of Batons shows that hesitancy leads to failure. There is timidity and a failure of nerve. Trying to cover up something which is false or lacks any real substance will be exposed as a fraud.

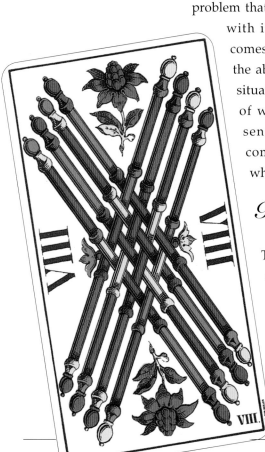

Eight of Batons

Keynote – Activity
Number Symbolism – Totality

The message of this card is to do with timing. The Eight of Batons indicates that this is a time for great activity. It does not bring success but suggests that the right path is being taken through the expenditure of effort. Opportunities must be grasped and initiatives taken, in order to push through to a satisfactory conclusion. This is a time of furious activity when everything seems to happen at once. Connections are made sparking off activity and energy. There is much coming and going, people making communications of all kinds. There may be travel opportunities in the air with the need to explore beyond the boundaries of everyday life.

Cooperation and understanding will come from others caught up in this maelstrom of activity. Enthusiasm is infectious and is encouraged by the speed at which things are now made to happen. There are no delays as progress is made at full steam ahead.

Reversed Meaning

Wasted energy is the order of the day now. No forethought is given before acting, with the conclusion that activity based on rush, rush, rush, is a complete waste of time. Despite the appearance of activity, nothing is actually being achieved.

Nine of Batons

Keynote – Strength
Number Symbolism – Completion

The Nine of Batons should be interpreted as a situation of great strength. The questioner has arrived at a virtually unassailable position from which it would be extremely difficult to dislodge them. It is a position of stability giving a sense of being safe and secure. From this position, it is possible to create an impenetrable defence and also launch successful attacks.

Moving away from this position would not be a good thing in terms of losing the security, stability and strength which it creates. All actions should be taken while remaining rooted in it such that the situation can be maintained. From this position there need be no cause for concern regarding the difficulties and problems presented by other people. This position of strength cannot be overthrown, unless the questioner moves away from it. Security is needed, for the situation is surrounded by hidden enemies and the risk of conflict.

Reversed Meaning

The meaning now is that there is a refusal to budge from a situation; there is pig-headedness and an inability to adapt and change when it is appropriate to do so.

Ten of Batons

Keynote – A burden
Number Symbolism – Conclusion

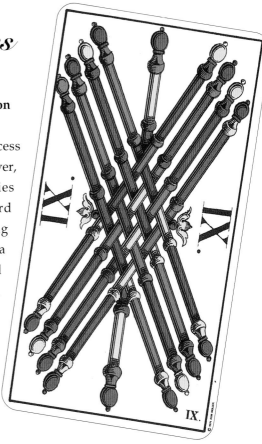

Power has been obtained, success achieved. The end result, however, is the burden that accompanies power and success. The card indicates that success is being misused. There is an abuse of a position that has been gained through luck and fate. This is a case of being handed something on a plate and then putting it to the wrong use. There is an element of tyranny at work here such that other people suffer from ones actions which are taken in an unfeeling way.

Power is being wielded for no reason other than its own self-expression. The repression thus caused creates a stagnant situation with all possibilities of future progress and development suppressed. The person creating this situation does not enjoy it and is themselves oppressed by the burden placed upon them. This card reveals the negative side of success and achievement.

Reversed Meaning

Power is being wielded ineffectually. No one is taking a blind bit of notice of the demands of a 'Little Dictator' who simply looks foolish to others. There is subterfuge planned to change this situation.

Making a Spread

Knight of Wands

VII   The Chariot

Nine of Swords

rmed with a knowledge of the Tarot pack, the meanings of the individual cards and the way the deck is structured and all held together, we can now proceed to work on making a reading. This chapter describes the ingredients required to do this – how to prepare the cards, how to lay them out in a 'spread' and how to create an effective reading.

There are many different spreads to try out and I have chosen the four most useful and easily accessible ones to start off with. Having mastered these, you can experiment with different ones and even create versions to suit your own needs. This chapter assumes that you have purchased your own Tarot pack by now, but if not you can refer to page 89 for advice on how to go about doing this.

Preparing for a Reading

Whichever spread you choose to use, the method for preparing the cards is the same. First, a question must be sought from the enquirer to put to the Tarot cards. A little time spent discussing the question to be put is often worth while because the question needs to be clear – an ambiguous or unclear question will simply lead to a muddled answer from the cards. Also, as you will discover, the type of question will influence your decision as to which is the most appropriate spread to use.

Before beginning the reading, it helps to set the right mood, perhaps with appropriate lighting, and even your favourite incense burning to enhance the atmosphere. The next step is to shuffle the cards. It does not matter how you do this, but I recommend placing the deck face down on a flat surface and swishing them around at random. This ensures that some cards will be reversed, appearing upside down in the reading. Shuffling by conventional methods does not allow for this to happen. While you are shuffling the cards, hold the question that is being asked clearly in your mind.

When the cards have been thoroughly shuffled, the diviner can cut the deck two or three times. Then the enquirer is invited to cut the cards once using their left hand.

Before beginning the reading, it helps to set the right mood.

Choosing a Significator

It is not always done, but it is often helpful to choose a 'significator' from the deck. This is a card which represents the enquirer themselves. It can be chosen when the enquirer cuts the deck, being taken from the top of the cut pile. This card may be kept to one side until later in the reading when it might be useful to consider it, depending on what the reading itself reveals.

Instead of choosing a card at random you may decide to choose a specific one, depending on the personality and characteristics of the enquirer. The Court cards are helpful for this purpose as they all represent different types of people. In general the four suits suggest the following.

Batons: a fair person with blue eyes
Cups: light brown hair and pale eyes
Coins: black hair and dark eyes
Swords: brown hair and brown eyes.

The cards are now ready for making your reading.

The Three-Card Spread

This is the simplest spread of all. It is also quick to prepare and can be highly effective. Three cards are chosen in turn from the top of the deck and are placed still face down in front of you, one to the left, one in the centre and one to the right. They can then be turned over to reveal the images that the fates have chosen in answer to the querent's question.

The card to the left (Card 1) represents the past. It indicates the events which have led up to the present situation and which have a direct bearing on the question being asked.

The card in the centre (Card 2) represents the present, the current situation with regard to the question being put.

The card to the right (Card 3) represents the future outcome – what the present situation is leading up to and how it will resolve.

Even if the question, as often happens, is simply about what will happen in the future, this spread is ideal, because the future results may only be properly understood by considering their connection with the present and the events which, in the past, have led up to these circumstances.

Remember that nothing in the Tarot is disconnected – in this case the emphasis should be put on the fact that past, present and future are all connected to one another.

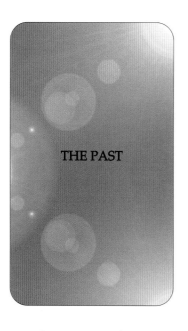

THE PAST

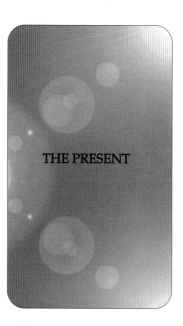

THE PRESENT

THE FUTURE

The Celtic Cross

The Celtic Cross spread is a comprehensive one which is probably the most used spread of all. It is suitable for use with questions which ask for an overall view of a situation. A general 'life reading' can be done using this spread. When considered as a whole, the Celtic Cross gives a clear view of the interconnected nature of all the factors which crop up in the reading.

The cards are prepared by shuffling and cutting in the usual way, then ten cards are selected in turn and placed face up according to the following pattern (see opposite).

Card 1 This card represents present circumstances. It also represents the questioner.

Card 2 This is positioned so that it lies right across card 1. It represents immediate obstacles. This card should always be interpreted with its upright meaning as you can see from its position that it is neither upright nor reversed but crosses Card 1. In fact it could be said to 'cross' the questioner.

Card 3 This is positioned above Card 1 and indicates the questioner's goal. It indicates the most that can be hoped for, based on current circumstances. It is the card which crowns the questioner.

Card 4 This is positioned below Card 1 and represents the events of the recent past, which are passing out of the questioner's life. They are still highly influential but are now below the surface.

Card 5 This is positioned to the left of Card 1 and indicates the events of the more distant past which are relevant to the current situation. They are events that have gone before the questioner.

Card 6 This is positioned to the right of Card 1 and represents the immediate future, events which are coming in to being – they are immediately in front of the questioner.

Four cards are now placed one above the other to the right of cards 1 to 6.

Card 7 This card represents the way that the querent's personality is affecting the situation and how they are expressing themselves.

Card 8 This is positioned above Card 7. It represents environmental factors, the influence of home, the places that the questioner visits, where he or she works.

Card 9 This is positioned above Card 8. It represents the questioner's hopes, if positioned upright, or fears if reversed.

Card 10 This is positioned above Card 9. It indicates the outcome of the situation. Given all the other factors revealed in the reading, this is where it is all leading to.

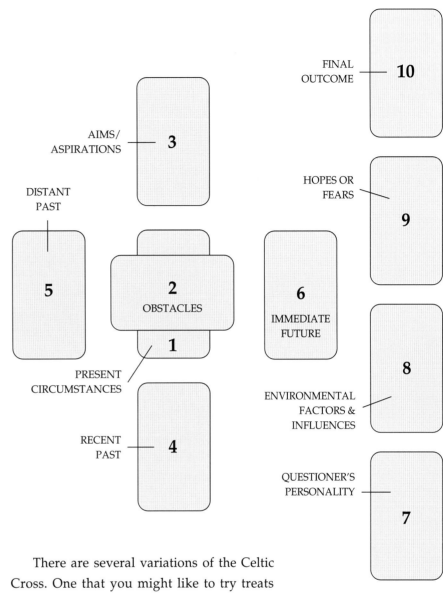

There are several variations of the Celtic Cross. One that you might like to try treats cards 7 to 10 differently. They can all be interpreted as representing the future. Card 7 is the immediate future, 8 is somewhat further away, 9 even further, while Card 10 represents the distant future. Some versions reverse the meaning of cards 5 and 6. I would choose what you feel most comfortable with and then stick to it consistently.

The Astrological Spread

There are two main versions of this particular spread. The first that I will describe is particularly suitable if a question is asked about the year ahead. In this version, when the pack has been prepared, 12 cards are chosen and they are placed in the sequence 1 to 12 as shown in the illustration. For this reading the cards are placed face up straight away. If a card is upright, its top will be towards the centre of the circle. If it is reversed, its bottom will be towards the centre.

Card 1 represents the month ahead. Card 2 represents the querent's circumstances two months ahead. Card 3 represents three months ahead, and so on.

Before commencing the reading, a thirteenth card is taken from the deck and this is placed in the centre of the circle face up. This is the significator which gives the overall tone of the reading and the year ahead. It is the most important card and should be interpreted first as it sets the tone for interpreting all the other cards.

In the next version of the Astrological Spread, the circle is set up in exactly the same way, however, the interpretation of the cards is different.

The circle of 12 cards, each representing a month of the year is a reminder of the 12 signs of the zodiac and of the 12 astrological houses. The houses represent different areas of life and it is these areas that are attributed to the 12 cards in this spread. They are as follows:

Card 1 This represents the querent, their image, the role that they play in life and the way that they like others to see them.

Card 2 This represents the querent's possessions, money and all personal material affairs.

Card 3 This represents brothers and sisters and their influence. It also represents short journeys and all methods of communication.

Card 4 This represents the home, the querent's roots and early influences.

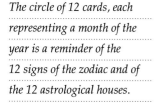

The circle of 12 cards, each representing a month of the year is a reminder of the 12 signs of the zodiac and of the 12 astrological houses.

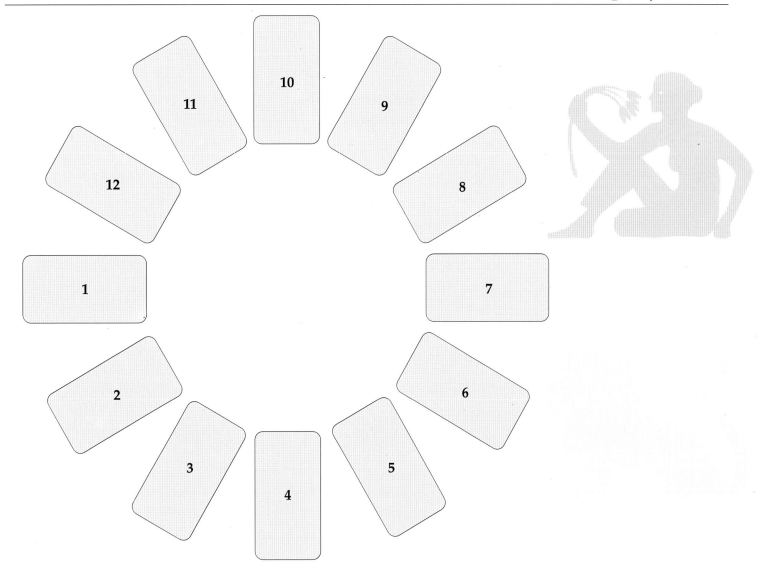

Card 5 This represents the querent's own children and the creative aspects of their life.

Card 6 This is the card of health and work and the way that the querent is helpful (or otherwise) to others.

Card 7 This represents personal partnerships.

Card 8 This represents the querent's involvement with other people's money. It is the card of death and birth and the process of regeneration. Wills and legacies may be indicated here.

Card 9 This represents teaching and learning, expanding horizons and the possibility of travel.

Card 10 This represents the querent's career or what it is they hope to achieve in life, their hopes and ambitions.

Card 11 This represents the querent's ideals and also their association with groups of people holding similar ideals, religious groups or political parties, for example.

Card 12 This shows those things that are hidden away in the querent's life. It may also show the sacrifices that need to be made.

Note that for both versions of the Astrological Spread, the cards are placed face up straight away. Not only does this mean that the cards can be treated in relationship to one another, but you can start your reading at any point on the circle, depending on the question that is asked. You don't need to progress round the cards in order, although you can if you wish to do so.

The Seven-Card Horseshoe Spread

This is a particularly useful spread to choose for giving guidance on a specific question or problem. After preparing the deck, seven cards are chosen and laid out in the pattern shown in the illustration. It is not important whether the cards are placed face up or down, but I prefer with this spread to keep them face down until they are interpreted.

Card 1 This describes the querent's past. It shows what influences are affecting the outcome of the question that has been put to the cards. It suggests to the querent those things from the past which might not have been thought relevant but which are. The card indicates past experiences which would now prove useful.

Card 2 This card indicates the present. It can be used to clarify the problem which might be worrying the querent. When compared with the previous card and the following one, it will be clear how things are moving, what changes are currently taking place and where the flow of events is leading to.

Card 3 This card indicates the future. Cards 1 and 2 are leading up to this one – you can see that there is a process of flow at work now as you consider the relationship between these three cards.

Card 4 This suggests the best course of action for the querent to take. Whether or not he or she will follow this advice is suggested by Cards 3 and 7 (the outcome).

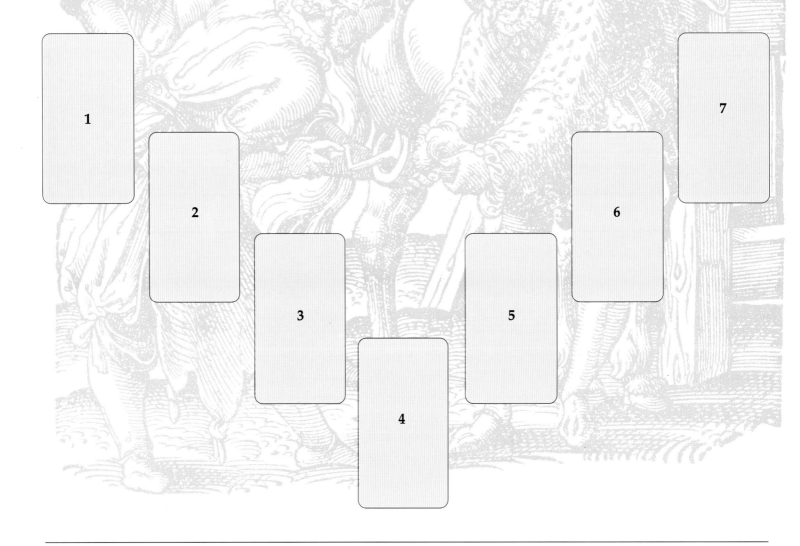

Card 5 This card represents the people surrounding the querent and the influence that they are having. It may show where support is coming from or, conversely, if the card is reversed, the obstacles that are being placed in the querent's way. This card reveals the feelings of other people and their influence.

Card 6 This is an indication of obstacles that are preventing the querent from achieving a satisfactory outcome. Even if the card suggests something quite positive, like contentment or happiness, this should still be interpreted as an obstacle (perhaps complacency in this case), although the degree of difficulties to be surmounted will need to be judged carefully.

Card 7 This is the outcome of the whole situation. If the querent were to accept the current situation and everything else that Cards 1 to 6 indicate, then the outcome is inevitable.

Eventually, the cards will begin to speak to you of their meaning.

Let The Question Decide

The fact that there are other spreads to try than the ones described above and also that it is common for each spread to have different versions, suggests that there is room for experiment. One of the most useful things to learn about the Tarot is that there are no hard and fast rules. Aim to have the confidence to interpret the cards according to your feelings and intuitions. Where the spreads are concerned, feel free to experiment with different versions of your own.

My own preference is to let the question decide which spread is most appropriate but the more you experiment with different ones and even with the same one, the more you will come to feel at home with your Tarot deck. Eventually, the cards will begin to speak to you of their meaning so that the text book descriptions take a back-seat role as you give your imagination free reign.

Tarot Workshop

*I*n this chapter we will use each of the spreads which were described in the previous chapter. The difference is that for each spread a particular question will be put to the Tarot and the subsequent reading will be described in full. This means that you can take part now by observing how all that has been presented to you so far can be used to make an interpretation. In each case, it is assumed that shuffling and the preparation work have been done.

The question being asked is given first, and there is an accompanying illustration to show which cards were drawn in response to the question and which positions they take up. The technique of interpretation is quite straightforward. It consists of first putting the meanings of the individual cards in a context appropriate to the question being asked and then to give an overall interpretation based on the general 'feel' of the cards as a whole.

The Three-Card Spread

Question: How will I fare in my job in the future?

Cards drawn:

    Card 1, the Lovers reversed
    Card 2, Eight of Swords
    Card 3, Five of Coins

Card 1 – the Past

The Lovers reversed indicates that when the job was taken up in the past the querent was not aware of what was being taken on. The job looked attractive but this was a veneer hiding the difficulties that would be encountered. It suggests that there was lack of realism in making a judgement about it and that hopes for a successful job would not be fulfilled.

Card 2 – the Present

The Eight of Swords indicates that any difficulties or adversity at work will be approaching an end. Difficult circumstances are persisting but it is clear that they are soon to be over, provided responsibilities can be faced up to and dealt with. Changes for the better are underlying the trouble and strife that is quite clearly in the open. It suggests that even though events may seem to conspire against the querent, it is well worth persisting with hard work and diligence

because all will soon transform into much better circumstances.

Card 3 – the Future

Leading on from the Eight of Swords, the Five of Coins (or Pentacles) will bring much worry in the future about money and the possible loss of employment. However, this card signifies a period of great activity when all the difficulties of the past have a chance to be dealt with and put behind one, as new opportunities arise and new directions open up. The card signifies new life arising from out of a period of turmoil and activity.

Summary

Finally, by considering the three cards together, it is clear that the general feeling of the reading is that, despite the present job being one which perhaps should not have been entered into in the first place, there is an opportunity in the present and the near future to deal with all the different problems and difficulties that have arisen as a result of bad decisions made in the past. Facing up to this task will mean that new avenues and opportunities will eventually open up. It is therefore advisable that the querent face up to current responsibilities and problems to ensure a much better future.

The Celtic Cross

Question: My life seems to have lost direction. Can you suggest what I should do?

Cards drawn:

Card 1, Judgement
Card 2, Seven of Swords
Card 3, Nine of Cups reversed
Card 4, Ten of Swords
Card 5, The Sun
Card 6, Justice
Card 7, Nine of Coins reversed
Card 8, Six of Coins
Card 9, The Chariot
Card 10, The Moon

Card 1 – The Present Situation

Judgement indicates that the time has come for a firm decision to be made right away. Where options might have been open in the past it is time now to steer along one particular route. The card indicates a final outcome from previous deeds and that a new phase of life is about to begin.

Card 2 – Crossing the Situation

The Seven of Swords suggests opposition to the current situation. Lack of awareness of ones own motives results in conflict with others. The card asks that you become aware of your inner feelings and needs.

Card 3 – The Questioner's Goal

The Nine of Cups reversed reveals that the querent is too optimistic about what can be achieved and this will be the result of listening to other people who are supportive while knowing that what they suggest is not possible. Beware of being damned by faint praise.

Card 4 – Recent Past

The Ten of Swords means that the worst has now past, that things can only get better, given that the right course of action is taken. This accords with the other cards read so far, in that the reading is pointing to new life based on a firm decision taken as soon as possible.

Card 5 – Distant Past

The Sun shows that the querent has, in the past, developed a strong sense of purpose in life but, taking other cards into account, this has got lost somewhere along the way. As this card is directly relevant to the current situation it suggests that this sense of purpose must be regained.

Card 6 – Immediate Future

Justice signifies that the querent is going to make the right decision and that the result will be a reordered situation that is favourable and brings the results that the questioner will feel they deserve.

Card 7 – Querent's Personality

The Nine of Coins reversed means that the questioner has been less than honest with other people and with themselves. Self-satisfaction is highly inappropriate – particularly as it is coupled with the over-optimism of Card 3. Devious means for obtaining goals result in destructive circumstances and this is therefore an area of concern.

Card 8 – Environmental Factors

The Six of Coins emphasizes the need to shift from self-gratification to assisting others. Generosity is called for and it might indeed be the key to the whole situation. If someone has been asking for assistance then it should be provided. This will involve the material affairs of someone who is close to the querent, either at home or at work.

Card 9 – Hopes

(Remember that this card would represent the querent's fears, if reversed.) The Chariot reveals that the questioner is hoping for a complete change of circumstances resulting from the winning of a battle or the successful outcome of dealing with a challenge. There are no half measures indicated here but that the questioner is quite prepared to accept all or nothing.

Card 10 – The Outcome

The Moon really confirms all that has gone before – that the current situation will change, that life will move on to a new phase. The questioner will find themselves in tune with their inner world of feelings and emotions such that they feel much much better about the new life which will come to them.

Summary

It should be clear how all of the cards in this reading fall into a pattern which suggests first the loss of a situation when the querent felt a strong sense of purpose in life, then the fighting of battles which has led to unhappiness and the urge to make changes. The time has come to make a firm decision, the decision taken will be the right one and will result in a happy outcome. The querent must be honest with themself and others, and should exhibit generosity to those that they are in a position to help.

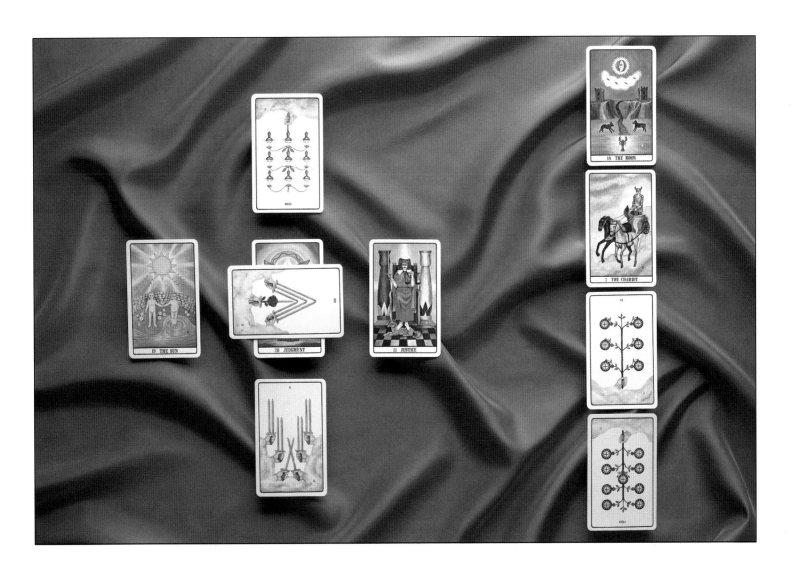

The Astrological Spread

Question: *Can you give me a reading which covers the year ahead?*

Cards drawn:

      Card 1, Four of Batons reversed
      Card 2, Queen of Swords
      Card 3, Eight of Coins
      Card 4, Ten of Coins
      Card 5, Two of Coins
      Card 6, Two of Cups
      Card 7, King of Cups
      Card 8, Page of Batons reversed
      Card 9, Ace of Cups reversed
      Card 10, Knight of Swords
      Card 11, The Tower reversed
      Card 12, Ace of Swords.

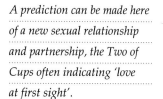

A prediction can be made here of a new sexual relationship and partnership, the Two of Cups often indicating 'love at first sight'.

Card 1 – First Month

The Four of Batons reversed means that the coming month will bring lack of support from other people. Assistance is withdrawn. The reason for this is that the querent's behaviour is found to be difficult by other people. The questioner comes across as superior and must beware that there is a tendency to become cut off from the realities of life.

Card 2 – Second Month

The Queen of Swords indicates that the querent will meet an important and influential woman. If the questioner is seen by her in a favourable light then she will bring much of benefit, being able to wield her power to the questioner's advantage. Such a person should be treated with respect in order to win her favour.

Card 3 – Third Month

The Eight of Coins reveals that this month will bring a change of fortune for the better. Money or material reward of some kind is indicated and hard work during this time will be well worth while. In fact, financial or material fortune will come as a direct result of hard work so the questioner should plan to be in a position to do this.

Card 4 – Fourth Month

The Ten of Coins continues the trend for financial gain. Family matters are indicated here and the movement of wealth from one person to another. Blood-ties are the important factor in the gaining of wealth. This could well be a time of accepting responsibility passed on from an older member of the family (or conversely for passing on responsibility to a younger member, if appropriate).

Card 5 – Fifth Month

The Two of Coins is a card of movement and change suggesting that the querent should plan to make changes at this time. Changes will be necessary to ensure continuing prosperity. Any resistance to change will bring misfortune. The card appears when new and unforeseen circumstances are present.

Card 6 – Sixth Month

The Two of Cups heralds the making of a new partnership. This will be a time for making new bonds, burying old disagreements and the creation of a happy partnership based on mutually beneficial circumstances. A prediction can be made here of a new sexual relationship and partnership, the Two of Cups often indicating 'love at first sight'. Could it be the woman who first appeared in the Second Month?

A relationship on which the querent depended for future security will end – perhaps the relationship was very one-sided in the first place, an unrequited love.

Card 7 – Seventh Month

The King of Cups indicates an encounter with a powerful man, someone who has the ability to change the querent's life. However, this man will play his cards close to his chest and it will be difficult to fathom his motives. It would be advisable to treat him with care because his outer manner will not give any real clues as to what his motives are.

Card 8 – Eighth Month

The Page of Batons reversed brings a warning. There will be malicious gossip and bad news in the air. The questioner should be careful about what he or she believes to be true. Malicious information will be presented but the purpose of it is to destabilize a situation, to create havoc and bring about the querent's downfall. Great care should be taken in making judgements based on what other people say.

Card 9 – Ninth Month

The Ace of Cups reversed unfortunately suggests the failure of a relationship. This may or may not be welcome but the questioner will lose much at this time and will feel despair and suffer from a loss of faith. A relationship on which the querent depended for future security will end – perhaps the relationship was very one-sided in the first place, an unrequited love.

Card 10 – Tenth Month

The Knight of Swords indicates a confrontation lies ahead – a battle which must be fought. It will be important for the querent not to go charging straight in, though, as forethought and planning are required if the outcome is to be successful. The querent will need to fight for something that he or she believes in and will be asked to rise to the occasion.

Card 11 – Eleventh Month

The Tower reversed is a fortunate card indicating that at this time a disaster will be averted at the last minute. The previous month indicates planning for coming turmoil and now the battle has been turned from one of defeat to a victory. It is even possible that the battle might not even be fought at all, although the situation can be described as a cliff-hanger!

Card 12 – Twelfth Month

The Ace of Swords ensures that the coming year ends on a triumphant note. It is a strong indicator of success and victory. It represents a hard-won breakthrough and the creation of a new order. Great changes can be expected at this time, changes which herald a new and successful phase of life.

Summary

It looks as if the questioner is in for a year of ups and downs. The early part of the year brings a new relationship which sparks off a period of gaining in wealth. However, this relationship, strong though it might be does not look set to last. Then a man enters the scene who could cause much disruption, stirring things up in a way which may well be unwelcome. However, despite early gains and then losses, the year ends on a most positive note after the possible disaster resulting from a conflict has been averted at the last minute.

The Seven-Card Horseshoe Spread

Question: *I have been offered a new business partnership. Should I enter into it?*

Cards drawn:

      Card 1, Queen of Batons
      Card 2, Seven of Cups
      Card 3, Two of Batons
      Card 4, Knight of Batons
      Card 5, Five of Swords
      Card 6, Page of Coins reversed
      Card 7, The Stars.

Card 1 – the Past

The Queen of Batons is the influence of a strong woman in the past who has brought creativity and productivity into the querent's life. This person has a relevance to the current question and she would be well worth involving in some way. If this woman is indeed the person offering the new partnership then this is an extremely positive card with which to begin the reading.

Card 2 – the Present

The Seven of Cups indicates that there are several possibilities open to the querent at present and not just a single choice. The right choice to make from these possibilities is not obvious but if taken will lead to great success. The card is suggesting that the querent should be aware that there is more than one way to skin a cat.

Card 3 – the Future

The Two of Batons brings the acceptance of a new role and new responsibilities. It brings the mantle of power and success which can only be worn with boldness and courage. It would seem that, so far in the reading, accepting this new partnership opportunity would be the right course of action, assuming that all other avenues are considered properly too.

Card 4 – the Best Course of Action

The Knight of Batons has a clear message, that an opportunity should be grasped quickly before it is too late. Taking this opportunity will bring a chance for change and once the opportunity is taken the changes will come quickly. There may also be an opportunity to travel or move to a different location.

Card 5 – Influential People

The Five of Swords brings to the attention of the querent that there are people involved in this situation who have nothing to offer. Following their lead would only result in movement up a dead end. It is therefore important that the questioner follows a different route than that offered by such people, or defeat and stagnation will result. The querent should swallow their pride and accept that some routes on offer will only lead to failure.

Card 6 – Obstacles

The Page of Coins reversed suggests that the querent may be stuck in the mentality of believing him or herself to be more important than is the case. There may be resistance to change based on a belief that the current situation is more important than it actually is.

Card 7 – The Stars

The Stars bring the final confirmation that a new partnership would be the right choice to make for it is the card which brings a bright future and that great things can be achieved. The fruits of success can be enjoyed during a period of calm and tranquillity. The querent has the blessing of the gods.

Summary

It becomes clear from considering the cards as a whole that the new partnership in question is a good thing and will bring much prosperity. Two important factors should be taken into account by the questioner. First, there are other avenues worth considering that may not have been obvious. There is not simply one choice only that can be taken here. Secondly, a decision must be made quickly, confidently and with no hesitation, for otherwise the opportunity will be lost.

Relationships and Interpretations

These four examples give an overall view of what can be achieved from a Tarot reading. Always put an emphasis in your interpretations on the general feeling of the reading and on the relationships between the cards.

You will see from the above that there is a lot more that could be said based on the cards which appear, but the interpretations that are presented above give the outlines which can

then be filled in. What you would fill them in with depends on other factors such as the age, sex and circumstances of the querent. The cards have to be interpreted to fit the situation and the person that presents themselves to you. You will find that the cards and their meanings only spring completely to life when you are reading for a real person and taking into account their unique personal circumstances.

Helpful Hints

Congratulations. You are now a fully-fledged Tarot card reader! It only remains to put your skill to good use and in this final chapter some ideas will be given as to your future direction. You will have discovered by now that there is much depth in the Tarot both in terms of its history and its effectiveness as an oracle. Having learnt to read the cards, assuming that you wish to develop your skill further, be assured that there is much that you can still learn. You will develop your skill in time simply through experience, but there are also some different directions that you could explore that you may not have thought of. It is these other possibilities that will be described in this final chapter. As an introduction, I want to go right back to the beginning to help you to decide which particular cards are right for you.

Choosing a Pack

Before reading this book, you may well have owned a Tarot deck, or with enthusiasm bought one straight away. This is fine and whatever the deck is that you have obtained will be appropriate for use with this book. However, if you have been more restrained and read the book first, or have decided that you would like to try a different pack of cards, then read on.

There is no difference between the different Tarot packs in terms of the number of cards, the structure, the basic interpretations of each card, etc. The main difference is simply to do with the style of the artwork, the different representations of the images and symbols. So, in choosing a deck you should be guided simply by your preference for the images, for the 'feel' of the cards. Go with your intuition to select the pack that you are drawn to.

There is a difficulty here in that the decks are usually sealed in clear film for the reason that you will want to be assured that the one you buy has not been handled by someone else. However, you can usually get a good idea of the style of the cards from the illustration on the outer box. You will find that many of the decks have specific books associated with them and these will have illustrations of the cards, but usually in black and white.

This book contains colour illustrations from several different Tarot decks which I have found are quite suitable for both a beginner's use and for a more advanced student.

A final point here is that it is a tradition in Tarot circles that you do not buy your own pack, but someone else obtains it for you. Whether or not you follow this tradition is up to you.

Tarot Etiquette

Another commonly observed Tarot etiquette is that you do not allow anyone else to handle your cards, except when preparing a reading and the questioner cuts the deck for you. As with all such ideas, it is up to you how far you take this. It does help you to develop a special relationship with your Tarot deck and develop a sense of care and even reverence for it. Some people like to talk in terms of psychic 'energies' and suggest that if someone else handles your cards then their energy will affect them and will become muddled up with your own.

To enhance this attitude of care for your cards, keep them in a special bag. Velvet or silk are the usual materials to use, but again anything appropriate will do.

Remember that when someone asks you for a reading, they may be unsure what the Tarot is all about and what you will actually do with it. It is well worth spending a little time at the beginning of a reading explaining what the Tarot is and how you are going to use it. This helps to put the querent at ease and assures them that there is no occult magic involved. Also, during a reading it is helpful for the querent to respond to your interpretations and make comments so that you can put your predictions in a personal context for them. Putting them at their ease right at the beginning of a reading helps to

Go with your intuition to select the pack that you are drawn to – there are many to choose from.

Counselling with the Tarot

There are three common situations that you will encounter. First, you will be interested in reading the Tarot for yourself. Second, you will do readings for people who are simply curious about the Tarot. But third, especially when your reputation as a reader spreads, most people who ask for a reading will do so because they have a particular difficulty that they would like guidance on.

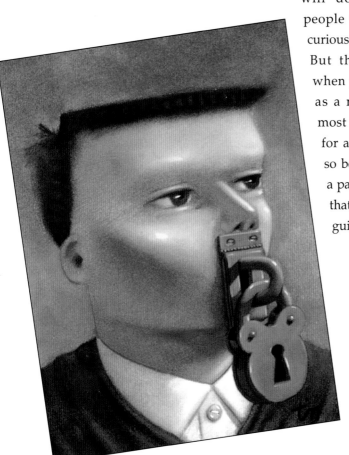

Because people may come to you with their personal problems seeking guidance, you should be aware that, in order to be a successful reader, you will need to have the ability to counsel people sensitively, based on what you see in the cards. For example, you may see or intuit something which you are not sure if it would be a good thing to tell the querent at this time. You must be aware of the necessity to decide how much to say, when to be completely open and when to hold back. The cards won't help you in this. It is a skill in handling people that you will need to develop.

Coupled with this is that you may be taken into the querent's confidence about private matters and it is important that you decide right from the outset that you will respect this privacy. After doing a reading, don't immediately rush out and tell your friends what passed between you and your client. There is no written code of conduct for Tarot readers, but there should perhaps be one.

You may be taken into the querent's confidence about private matters and it is important that you decide right from the outset that you will respect this privacy.

Tricks of the Trade

Sorry to disappoint you but there are none! I suppose if there is a trick it is to be quite clear that there is nothing to hide about the Tarot cards and that the process of reading the Tarot is a natural one – there is nothing to fear in the cards. Others may be astounded at how accurate your readings are but the trick is not to become swollen-headed at this and proclaim yourself as having mystical powers. Be quite down to earth and keep things in perspective.

Be careful also neither to make your readings too short nor too long. If too short, then your interpretations will be superficial. If too long, they will become boring and much of the information will not be absorbed by the person you are reading for. Try to avoid giving lectures and endless wise advice, a common fault with many Tarot readers.

I suppose the main trick is in making the right judgement about not only what to say but how much to say too. Be constantly aware of the effect that your interpretations are having and through this awareness you will know whether or not to probe further or move onto a different tack.

Tarot Meditations

And now we come on to some of the different ways that the Tarot can be used. Meditating on the different cards is an excellent way of learning what they are all about but it has other benefits too.

Try taking each card from the Major Arcana in turn and living with it for a day or so. Keep it somewhere where you can see it. Think about it every now and again and keep some notes of the thoughts that occur to you about it. Contemplate the card and you will be amazed at the insights that come to you.

Don't worry about the usual meaning of the card. Based on your meditations, come up with your own interpretation of its significance. This may be similar to the textbook description or it may be different. It doesn't matter. The point is to let the image on the card work its effect on your unconscious mind. This will in return throw up images and ideas that connect with the card and give you insights about it.

You will find that it is not only an enjoyable experience to work through the cards in this way but that it reveals all sorts of new connections and insights, not only about the cards but about yourself too.

Inner Exploration

Now try taking the meditative process a stage further. Make yourself comfortable somewhere that you won't be interrupted, close your eyes and picture the image from one of the Tarot cards in the Major Arcana, or perhaps one of the Court cards. Use your imagination and let the card come to life. For example, if you are visualizing the King of Cups, first picture the card and then imagine that the King of Cups comes alive in your imagination so that he can move around the scene that you have imagined.

The value of this is that you can now communicate with this particular card, holding an inner dialogue with the figure on it. In this way you will gain even more insights about the meaning of the card and its significance for you.

The idea of doing this might be a bit uncomfortable and if so don't try it. Some people may find it difficult to do, having perhaps not used their imagination since they were children. However, it is a perfectly natural thing to do. The process is similar to daydreaming except that you have chosen a particular subject for the object of your waking dream.

If this approach appeals to you, it is worth exploring further and finding out more about this process of inner exploration, or 'active imagination' as it is sometimes called. Again you are setting up a two-way process whereby you learn about the meaning of the card but also it will reveal to you facets of your own inner self.

Contemplate the card and you will be amazed at the insights that come to you.

Close your eyes and picture the image from one of the Tarot cards in the Major Arcana, or perhaps one of the Court cards. Use your imagination and let the card come to life.

A Group Reading

It may not have occurred to you but it is certainly possible to do a Tarot reading to throw light on any question about the past, present and future. For example, it is possible to prepare a reading to describe a particular company, a project of some sort, the affairs of a group of people and even of a country. Institutions and associations of all shapes and sizes are fair game. The Tarot can also be useful in determining trends of all sorts, economic for example.

It is an interesting experiment to perform a Tarot reading for a group of people, perhaps one with a common purpose so that you can ask the Tarot about the prospects for the success of the group. Instead of reading for yourself or for one other person, reading for several with a common purpose or question has the added advantage that there are several minds at work and involved, so that one person may see the relevance of one card and situation, whereas another will see something different or leading in another direction. The issues that a group reading brings out can be quite inspiring and certainly provide much material for discussion.

The issues that a group reading brings out can be quite inspiring and certainly provide much material for discussion.

Developing Intuition

If during a reading you can allow the cards to speak through you in the way described above, opening yourself to allow your imagination to work in response to them, you will find that your readings are that much more powerful and effective. Intuition and even psychic abilities are encouraged by this process. What you are doing is allowing your unconscious mind to respond to the images on the cards. The thoughts, feelings and images which then arise in you as a result of this are valuable in amplifying the meaning of the cards and even help you to interpret well beyond the obvious surface meanings of the cards.

I mentioned earlier that half of doing a Tarot reading is allowing your imagination and intuition to have its say, so that you only use the traditional meanings of the cards as a starting point, as a hook for their deeper significance. The key is to trust yourself and your intuition. You won't go far wrong as long as you keep within the context that the cards are expressing. Learn the rules and then forget them!

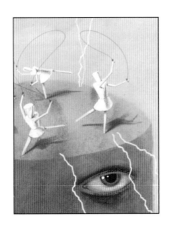

What you are doing is allowing your unconscious mind to respond to the images on the cards.

Tarot Fantasy

Your Tarot cards will give back to you what you put into them. The more attention that you give to them, the more they will repay you. Their value and use is only limited by your imagination so give this full reign both during your readings and when learning about or exploring the cards.

There is no reason why eventually you should not create your own Tarot pack, especially if you have an artistic temperament and like to express yourself in images. Paintings and even music have been inspired by the Tarot, so you will be working in a great tradition here too.

If you decide to create your own Tarot cards, you could include elements from different packs that appeal to you and use the outline illustrations as a guideline.

One aspect of the Tarot that I have not mentioned is colour. Colour symbolism is significant and not many decks take this into account. However, this is a subject well worth exploring and knowing what the different colours represent will be helpful in creating the right mood and meanings in your own creative artwork. Drawing or painting the results of your Tarot meditations is also a further way of developing your intuitive skills and therefore your ability to use the Tarot successfully.

In Conclusion

Above all, have fun with your Tarot, probing the mysteries of time and the universe. Anyone, with a little effort, can read the Tarot well, and as we have seen there is much more to it than meets the eye. In using your Tarot cards you will not only be able to help others with their problems and difficulties, no matter how great or small, but you will be embarking on a great exploration. You will be discovering how the past, present and future are all connected, can all be reflected in the symbols on the cards.

I believe that the main contribution that the Tarot cards can make is in helping us to understand a little better who we are and what our lives are all about. By helping us to achieve this, the Tarot can be a guide to making our lives that much more worth living.

Finally, it only remains for me to suggest that you take your cards, give them a good shuffle and see what crops up for you.

Happy reading.

In using your Tarot cards you will not only be able to help others with their problems and difficulties, no matter how great or small, but you will be embarking on a great exploration.

Glossary

Divination Consulting an oracle such as the Tarot with regard to future events.

Elements The astrological groups of signs of the zodiac – Earth, Water, Fire and Air, each of which corresponds with a Tarot suit.

Major Arcana These are the 'greater' cards of the Tarot pack, consisting of 21 numbered cards, and one which is unnumbered. This is the Fool, which sometimes appears first and sometimes last in the order of the Major Arcana. The Fool is sometimes numbered '0'.

Minor Arcana These are the 'lesser' cards of the Tarot pack, consisting of the four suits – Swords, Coins (or Discs), Staves (or Batons) and Cups. Each suit consists of ten numbered or 'pip' cards and four Court Cards – King, Queen, Knight and Knave (or Page).

Numerology Number symbolism.

Oracle Any system for predicting the future.

Querent or Questioner The person who seeks to have a question answered by the Tarot.

Reader The Tarot consultant or person who reads the cards.

Reversed card A Tarot card which appears upside down in a reading.

Significator A particular card representing either the querent or the overall situation described by a Tarot reading.

Spread The pattern in which the Tarot cards are placed when preparing a reading.

Trump card A card in the Major Arcana.

Further Reading

There are many books available for further reading, particularly as Tarot decks often have a specific book associated with them.

Here are some which are of a more general nature. Particularly recommended is the title by Alfred Douglas.

Anonymous, *Meditations on the Tarot*, Element

Douglas, Alfred, *The Tarot*, Arkana

Eason, Cassandra, *Tarot for Today's Woman*, Foulsham

Fenton, Sasha, *Tarot in Action*, Aquarian

Garen, Nancy, *Tarot Made Easy*, Piatkus

Mann, A.T., *The Elements of the Tarot*, Element

Summers, Catherine & Vayne, Julian, *Self-Development with the Tarot*, Foulsham

Walker, Ann, *Living Tarot*, Capall Bann

Index

This index will help you to locate quickly the meanings of any of the 78 cards in the Tarot pack. You will find this helpful when interpreting a spread of cards.

Acknowledgements
We would like to thank the following for generously supplying props for photography:
Jody Cole; Fired Earth; Bernard Hayes; Inner Light Design; Joy & Alistair MacDougall; David Markson; Past Times; Isabelle Mercedes Stanley-Moss; Treasure Chest.